TOP SECRET:

The FBI Files on
John Steinbeck

Also by Thomas Fensch . . .

Conversations with John Steinbeck

Steinbeck and Covici:
*The Story of a Friendship**

**republished by New Century Books*

Volumes in the Top Secret series
Published by New Century Books:

World War Two:
U.S. Military Plans for the Invasion of Japan

The FBI Files on Elvis Presley

The Vietnam War:
Confidential Files on the Siege and Loss of Khe Sanh

FBI Files on the Lindbergh Baby Kidnapping

CIA Files on the U-2 Plane Program, 1954–1974

The Kennedy–Khrushchev Letters

The FBI Files on John Steinbeck

TOP SECRET:

The FBI Files on John Steinbeck

Edited by Thomas Fensch

NEW CENTURY BOOKS

This book is dedicated to
Kenneth Kopel, Ph.D., Houston

with more gratitude
than any words can express . . .

New Century Books
P.O. Box 1205
Santa Teresa, New Mexico, 88008

Library of Congress number
2002094984

ISBN: 0-930751-52-3 Hardcover
ISBN: 0-930751-53-1 Paperback

Contents

Chronology:

Key dates in the life of John Steinbeck

The following is a general chronology of the career of John Steinbeck.

1902—John Steinbeck born in Salinas, California.

1920–1925—Steinbeck attends Stanford University, but fails to graduate.

1926–1929—Steinbeck lives in California, writing stories and novels.

1929—Steinbeck's first novel, *Cup of Gold,* published by Robert M. McBride & Co.

1932—Steinbeck's second novel, *The Pastures of Heaven,* published by Brewer, Warren and Putnam.

1933—Steinbeck's third novel, *To a God Unknown,* published by Robert O. Ballou.

1935—*Tortilla Flat* is published by Covici-Friede. It won the Commonwealth Club of California Gold medal.

1936—Covici-Friede publishes *In Dubious Battle.* It wins another Gold Medal from the Commonwealth Club of California.

1937—Covici-Friede publishes *Of Mice and Men*

as novel and play and *The Red Pony.*

1938—Covici-Friede dissolved. Pascal Covici joins The Viking Press as senior editor. The Viking Press publishes *The Long Valley.*

1939—The Viking Press publishes *The Grapes of Wrath.*

1940—Steinbeck awarded a Pulitzer Prize for *The Grapes of Wrath.*

1941—The Viking Press publishes *Sea of Cortez,* by Steinbeck and Ricketts, and *The Forgotten Village.*

1942—The Viking Press publishes Steinbeck's *The Moon Is Down* and *Bombs Away.*

1945—The Viking Press publishes *Cannery Row.*

1947—The Viking Press publishes *The Wayward Bus* and *The Pearl.*

1948—The Viking Press publishes *A Russian Journal.*

1950—The Viking Press publishes *Burning Bright* as novel and playscript.

1951—The Viking Press publishes Steinbeck's *The Log from the Sea of Cortez,* with preface about Ed Ricketts.

1952—The Viking Press publishes *East of Eden.*

1954—The Viking Press publishes *Sweet Thursday.*

1957—The Viking Press publishes *The Short Reign of Pippin IV.*

1958—The Viking Press publishes *Once There Was a War.*

1961—The Viking Press publishes *The Winter of Our Discontent.*

1962—John Steinbeck wins The Nobel Prize for Literature. The Viking Press publishes

Travels with Charley in Search of America.

1964—Pascal Covici dies.

1966—The Viking Press publishes *America and Americans*, edited by Thomas Guinzburg.

1968—John Steinbeck dies.

1969—The Viking Press publishes *Journal of a Novel: The East of Eden Letters.*

1975—The Viking Press publishes *Steinbeck: A Life in Letters*, edited by Elaine Steinbeck and Robert Wallstein.

1976—Farrar, Straus and Giroux publishes Steinbeck's *The Acts of King Arthur and His Noble Knights.*

Introduction

The FBI Files on John Steinbeck is the seventh volume in the Top Secret Series of formerly-secret government files, published by New Century Books.

This volume begins with a short memorandum from then Attorney General Francis Biddle, to FBI Director J. Edgar Hoover, with a note from Steinbeck:

> Do you suppose you could ask Edgar's boys to stop stepping on my heels? They think I'm an enemy alien . . .

This is nothing in the Steinbeck file prior to that memo from Biddle and the Steinbeck note, written in New York City, presumably just prior to Biddle's memo to J. Edgar Hoover, which was dated May 11, 1942 (except for a clip about a California extortion attempt).

J. Edgar Hoover steadfastly denied, over the years, that the FBI had ever investigated Steinbeck; Hoover's denials were, at the very least disingenuous, at worst, an outright lie.

Although there is nothing in the FBI files prior to the Biddle to Hoover memo in May, 1942, earlier letters, memos and records could have easily been discarded, to "prove" Hoover's statement that the FBI had never investigated Steinbeck.

In fact, the FBI may well have been involved in the investigation by the governmental agency, G-2, which formally stated that Steinbeck was unfit to be an officer in the U.S. Armed Forces. That decision was made despite the California agent-of-record's recommendation that Steinbeck was of good character, intelligence and clearly capable of being an officer in the armed forces, during World War Two.

Steinbeck may have known that G-2 was investigating him as an officer candidate and presumably believed the FBI was involved.

(Steinbeck spent the war as a correspondent and published the book, *Bombs Away: the Story of a Bomber Team* (1942) and, years later, in 1958, published his war correspondence under the title, *Once There Was a War.* These books are now two of Steinbeck's least republished titles.)

In these files are citizen complaints about Steinbeck's books, files of the G-2 investigation, which the FBI referred to, in later years, and reviews of evaluations of Steinbeck's publications.

The FBI repeatedly up-dated profiles on Steinbeck, using anonymous citizen complaints and occasional reviews of his work.

The FBI also acted as clearinghouse for Steinbeck files; FBI agents in specific bureaus reported to Washington when Steinbeck entered the country; records from other governmental agencies were filed at the FBI and the FBI frequently sent copies of their records to other agencies asking for background material on

Steinbeck.

In 1954, a summary was sent from the FBI to the U.S.I.A. (United States Information Agency) with the following first sentence:

> No investigation has been conducted by this Bureau concerning the above-named individual. A review of the files, however, reflects that in May, 1945, a reliable source . . .

Files occasionally mention references to *The Daily Worker,* the Communist newspaper. However, reactions to Steinbeck's books by communist leaders and publications were, over the years, mixed. The communist press generally approved of Steinbeck's California novels such as *The Grapes of Wrath and In Dubious Battle,* but did not appreciate his post-World War Two books such as *A Russian Journal,* which was, in fact, out-of-date as soon as it was printed.

In 1940, John Steinbeck won the Pulitzer Prize for *The Grapes of Wrath* and in 1962, Steinbeck won the Nobel Prize for literature, one of the very few Americans to win the Nobel Prize for literature. But throughout the years, the FBI files mention vague references to communist organizations, approval of Steinbeck's work by the communist press and, of course, denial by G-2 of Steinbeck's character as an officer candidate during World War Two.

Were "Edgar's boys" on Steinbeck's heels, as he claimed in 1942? Clearly personnel from G-2 were. Did Steinbeck confuse FBI agents with G-2 personnel? Probably. Were there records in the

Steinbeck file prior to the Biddle-Hoover correspondence that begins this file? After some 60 years, there is now no proof.

Were there other records in the Steinbeck file not now open to public view? New Century Books advises that original documents make no reference to other such letters withheld from this archive during the years in question, but that still may be the case.

Every effort has been made to accurately reprint these letters, memos, files and data, however many of the letters are very dark and neither New Century Books nor the editor can completely guarantee the accuracy of the dates, or names or other phrases reproduced in this book. Sections of pages which have been *redacted* (blacked out prior to release to the public) are indicated in the text; some of the pages which have redactions are shown in the Appendix.

Note: Many pages shown in the Appendix are faint (or illegible) because of the age of the original file pages and because these pages had to be photocopied and then recopied and reduced for publication. These pages are included to show the contents of a variety of FBI file pages and to also show the *redactions* prior to release to the public. Every effort has been made to reproduce contents accurately, from full-sized FBI document pages.

— Thomas Fensch

TOP SECRET:

The FBI Files on
John Steinbeck

The first major item in the FBI Steinbeck file is this short note from Francis Biddle, Attorney General to FBI Director J. Edgar Hoover. Note that Biddle calls Steinbeck "the playwright":

May 11, 1942

MEMORANDUM FOR MR. HOOVER

Will you note the attached letter of John Steinbeck, the playwright?

Francis Biddle
Attorney General

Steinbeck's short letter ("Do you suppose you could ask Edgar's boys . . .) to Biddle was typically Steinbeck:

(There is no reference in the files what "Congratulations on the S.S. matter" might have referred to; presumably it was a Secret Service operation.)

THE BEDFORD
118 East 40th Street
New York

Caledonia 5-1000

Dear Mr. Biddle:

I'm very sorry I haven't been able to see you. Do you suppose you could ask Edgar's boys to stop stepping on my heels? They think I'm an enemy alien. It's getting tiresome.

Congratulations on the S.S. matter.

John Steinbeck

J. Edgar Hoover replies to Biddle in this memo date-stamped May 21, 1942. If Hoover was being disingenuous in replying that the FBI had not been investigating Steinbeck, the FBI surely would do so in the future.

And if Steinbeck believed the FBI was following him in the past, they probably were, although there are no documents in the FBI files which have dates prior to the (above) Biddle-Hoover exchange.

May 21, 1942

MEMORANDUM FOR THE ATTORNEY GENERAL

Reference is made to your memorandum dated May 11, 1942, transmitting a letter addressed to you by John Steinbeck, in which Steinbeck complained that he was being investigated as an enemy alien by representatives of this Bureau.

I wish to advise that Steinbeck is not being and has never been investigated by this Bureau. His letter to you is returned herewith.

Respectfully,

John Edgar Hoover
Director

October, 1942, the Attorney General's office continues to follow up and ask for "the bureau's file on John Steinbeck."

The italic paragraph following the memo is FBI employee Stalcup's post script regarding the matter. E.A. Tamm was one of the higher FBI employees, reporting to Hoover and his associate Clyde Tolson.

October 27, 1942

MEMORANDUM FOR MR. E. A. TAMM

Miss Collins in the Attorney General's office telephoned and advised that the Attorney General wanted to see the Bureau's file on John Steinbeck tomorrow morning (Oct. 28th).

Respectfully,

D. Stalcup

5:45 P.M. Miss Collins was advised that the Bureau had conducted no investigation concerning John Steinbeck and her attention was called to the Bureau's memorandum of May 21, 1942, in which the Attorney General was so advised.

October 30, 1942: FBI employee Edward A. Tamm advises Hoover on the Steinbeck matter. The FBI and many others would continue to be offended by Steinbeck's series of newspaper articles about the Okies in California for the *San Francisco News* which was reprinted as the pamphlet "Their Blood is Strong." Steinbeck's reportage for *The San Francisco News* "proved" the validity of his novel *The Grapes of Wrath;* without his reportage, which was included in the novel, critics could have claimed that his novel had no bearing in fact.

Californians were so offended by *The Grapes of Wrath* that Steinbeck could never again live in his native state.

Steinbeck liked to claim that he followed Okie families from Oklahoma through the mountain west into California. The truth is that he met some families at the Nevada-California border and journeyed with them into the fruit lands of the Salinas area and the San Joaquin Valley.

The Joad family was a composite of several Okie families which Steinbeck met; such composites are beyond the pale, now, journalistically. Some reporters have been fired in recent years for publishing profiles which were later discovered to be composites.

October 30, 1942

MEMORANDUM FOR THE DIRECTOR

Re: John Steinbeck – Author

In response to her previous request I telephonically advised Miss Collins in the Attorney General's office that we had in our possession two pamphlets which concerned the above-entitled individual. One of these entitled "Their Blood is Strong," was written by the subject and published in 1938 by the Simon J. Lubin Society of California. The material in this pamphlet is similar to that contained in his book "The Grapes of Wrath" and concerns the activities of migratory agricultural workers. The other pamphlet, which was furnished to us in May, 1938, is entitled "Writers Take Sides" and contains the opinions of several hundred authors as to whether they are for or against Franco. I informed Miss Collins that the subject was one of the authors quoted therein and further advised her I would make these pamphlets available to her for whatever purpose she may need them. Miss Collins stated she would appreciate the use of them very much.

Respectfully,

Edward A. Tamm

December 3, 1942. A citizen of West Palm Beach, Florida writes to J. Edgar Hoover complaining about Steinbeck. Some of the letter has been *redacted* (legalese for *blacked out*) prior to the letter's release to the public through the Freedom of Information Act.

For further examples of citizen letters to J. Edgar Hoover, see: *The FBI Files on Elvis Presley*, passim.

December 3, 1942

Hon. J. Edgar Hoover,
Chief of F.B.I. Washington, D.C.

Subject: John Ernst Steinbeck
Complaint: Proposed agitation of Japanese Relocation Centers, California & West

Sir:

For some times past I have resented books by Steinbeck, for they portray such unrepresentative pictures of our American life in rural districts. I live near the Everglades farms district and most of the migrants out there live better than I do, while they are here for the picking season.

Steinbeck's name is John Ernst Steinbeck. His father was a German, born in Florida of German parents, according to the story in Who's Who in U.S. writing circles. But of course the author furnishes the information about himself.

My reason for writing this is that it is rumored that Steinbeck is now gathering information for a heart-throb about the sad condition of Japanese in Relocation Centers in the West. I think it would be best for all concerned that he be not permitted to issue such a story until after the war — if ever.

Under strict enforcement of postal regulations, Steinbeck's books would not be permitted to go through U.S. mails, because of their scurrilous and obscene passages. These are held up by the examples of the immoral life of the U.S. in foreign countries opposed to us. I understand his books have been translated into German and circulated as "horrible examples," but I cannot prove this.

> THIS LETTER DOES NOT NEED A REPLY. IT IS ONLY SENT TO YOU . . . . . . AS INFORMATION.

You may have all this information from other sources; but I will explain why I am writing it. During the other World War I made reports direct to [REDACTED] when they did not concern local matters, but came to my attention regarding other sections of the country. I had authority to do this.

Where is Mr. Steinbeck?

Is he attempting to get information concerning government housing of soldiers?

He might dress in uniform and hang around incomplete camps like Boca Ratons, trying to get information as to inadequacy of camps before they are completed and outfitted perfectly. I hope this will not occur.

Respectfully yours

December 19, 1942. Hoover passes on a summary of the West Palm Beach, Florida, citizen's letter to Dillon S. Myer, Director of the War Relocation Authority, in California:

December 19, 1942

To: Mr. Dillon S. Myer, Director, War Relocation Authority, Barr Building, Washington, D.C.

From: J. Edgar Hoover — Director, Federal Bureau of Investigation

Subject: John Ernst Steinbeck

For your information and whatever consideration you may deem advisable, there is set forth below the pertinent portion of a communication recently received at this Bureau from one [REDACTED] West Palm Beach, Florida

West Palm Beach, Florida

December 8, 1942

Hon. J. Edgar Hoover
Chief of F.B.I. Washington, D.C.

Subject: John Ernst Steinbeck

Complaint: Proposed agitation of Japanese Relocation Centers, California & West

Sir:

"For some time past I have resented books by Steinbeck, for they portray such unrepresentative pictures of our American life in rural districts. I live near the Everglades farms district and most of the migrants out there live better than I do, while they are here for the picking season.

Steinbeck's name is John Ernst Steinbeck. His father was a German, born in Florida of German parents, according to the story in Who's Who in U.S. writing circles. But of course the author furnishes the information about himself.

My reason for writing this is that it is rumored that Steinbeck is now gathering information for a heart-throb about the sad condition of Japanese in Relocation Centers in the West. I think it would be best for all concerned that he be not permitted to issue such a story until after the war — if ever.

The War Department transmits to J. Edgar Hoover the results of an extensive investigation of Steinbeck's character and decides that Steinbeck should "not be considered favorably for a commission in the Army of the United States."

The report, contains this paragraph:

ADVERSE INFORMATION:

1. Subject has associated with individuals who are known to have a radical political and economic philosophy, and with some members of the Community Party.

(These pages are reproduced in the Appendix.)

The end of the report, carrying the section

RECOMMENDATIONS: also includes a hand-written notation in the left bottom margin:

Subj (subject) previously disapproved for a Commission by War Dept. Personnel Board.

All these denials of Steinbeck's loyalty were made in opposition to the California agent, Martin Frankel's recommendation, which reads in part:

Three excellent sources of information — the Carmel Postmaster, Subject's attorney and subject's ex-wife — agree on these points:

1. Subject is not a communist.
2. Subject is loyal, patriotic, honest.
3. Subject is an excellent writer.
4. Subject would make a good officer if his writing ability is utilized.

The report, dated May 23, 1943, continues:

<u>AGENT'S NOTES:</u>

This Agent believes that Subject would pass the requisite of honesty, loyalty and integrity insofar as his commission in the United States Army is concerned. It is the question of whether Subject would be of more value as a civilian employee or an Officer that higher authorities must decide. If Subject is to be employed by the United States Army in positions in which his xxxx writing ability may be utilized, it is the opinion of this Agent that he should be commissioned.

TOP SECRET

MARTIN FRANKEL
Special Agent CIC

These pages are reproduced in the Appendix and they appear here as they appeared in the original Steinbeck file.

San Francisco, California
May 1, 1943,
Case No. IX-O/S-14305c.

MEMORANDUM FOR THE OFFICER IN CHARGE

Subject: John E. Steinbeck, aka Dr. Beckstein, 15041 Del Gado Drive, Sherman Oaks, California

Re: Police check.

On February 23, 1943, this Agent checked the records of the Office of Naval Intelligence, 12th Naval District, the American Legion Radical Research Bureau, the San Francisco Field Office of the Federal Bureau of Investigation, and the San Francisco Police Department, all of San Francisco, California, regarding Subject.

The Federal Bureau of Investigation and the San Francisco Police Department reported no record of Subject.

The Office of Naval Intelligence reported the following records

> "DIO files refer to one John STEINBECK, P.O. Box 321, Los Gatos, Calif., who was a subscriber to the PEOPLE'S WORLD as

of Sept., 1939. (It should be noted that John STEINBECK, the author, also maintained a home in Los Gatos)."

The American Legion Radical Research Bureau reported the following:

11/9—1936:	Was Pacific Weekly contributor. Red publication at Carmel.
11/15—1938:	One of the sponsors of the Assembly of Youth, January 9 and 10.
4/1—1938:	Contributed article in this issue of Pacific Weekly (Red publication) re: The Racial Prejudice Among the Agricultural Workers in California.
10/17:	Chairman of the newly formed Committee to Aid Agricultural Organisation. (Very Red outfit).
6/4—1939:	His book "The Grapes of Wrath" was branded as Red propaganda by Father A. D. Spearman, S. J., director of the library of Loyola, U.L.A.

His former wife, Carol Henning Steinbeck, was registered Communist, Santa Clara County — 1938 — while living at Rt. 1, Box 98-D, Los Gatos.

Nicholas Zavinsky, Special Agent, CIC.

CONFIDENTIAL

Salinas, California
May 26, 1943
Case No. IX-O/S-14305c.

MEMORANDUM FOR THE OFFICER IN CHARGE

Subject: John E. Steinbeck
425 Kardley Avenue
Pacific Grove, California

Re: Police Check

On May 26, 1943 this Agent checked the records of the Salinas Police Department, Salinas, California, the Carmel Police Department, Carmel, California, and the Monterey Police Department, Monterey, California in connection with the investigation of Subject, who is being considered for a commission in the Army of the United States.

Salinas, California Police Department . . . . . No Record

Carmel, California, Police Department . . . . . No Record

Monterey, California Police Department . . . . . No Record

MARTIN FRANKEL
Special Agent CIC

CONFIDENTIAL

Salinas, California
May 29, 1943
Case No. IX-O/S-14305c.

MEMORANDUM FOR THE OFFICER IN CHARGE

Subject: John E. Steinbeck
425 Kardley Avenue
Pacific Grove, California

Re: Covering Memorandum

Three excellent sources of information — the Carmel Postmaster, Subject's attorney, and Subject's ex-wife — agree on these points:

1. Subject is not a communist.
2. Subject is loyal, patriotic, honest.
3. Subject is an excellent writer.
4. Subject would make a good officer if his writing ability is utilized.

AGENT'S NOTES:

This Agent believes that Subject would pass the requisite of honesty, loyalty and integrity insofar as his commission in the United States Army is concerned. It is the question of whether Subject would be of more value as a civilian employee or an Officer that higher authorities must decide. If Subject is to be employed by the United States Army in positions in which his xxxx writing ability may be utilized, it is the opinion of this Agent that he should be commissioned.

MARTIN FRANKEL
Special Agent CIC

CONFIDENTIAL

San Francisco, California
11 June 1943
Case No. IX-O/S-14305c.

MEMORANDUM FOR THE OFFICER IN CHARGE

Subject: John E. Steinbeck
15041 Del Gado Drive
Sherman Oaks, California

Re: Police Check

On 8 June 1943 this Agent checked the records of the Sheriff's office, Santa Clara County, California and the Police Department, Los Gatos, California, regarding the Subject.

Police Department, Los Gatos . . . . . .

No Record.

Sheriff's Ofice, Santa Clara County . . . . . . No Record.

CHARLES O. SHIELDS
Agent, CIC

CONFIDENTIAL

San Francisco, California
June 14, 1943
Case No. IX-O/S-14305c.

MEMORANDUM FOR THE OFFICER IN CHARGE

SUBJECT: JOHN E. STEINBECK
15041 Del Gado Drive
Sherman Oaks, California

Re: Acquaintance check with Miss Barbara Burke

On June 9, 1943, this Agent interviewed MISS BARBARA BURKE, 3065 Jackson Street, San Francisco, California regarding Subject.

MISS BURKE bought the Subject's first house at Los Gatos and became intimately acquainted as the Subject lived on the premises for a short time thereafter. MISS BURKE believes Subject to be unquestionably loyal, having heard him say that he had never voted the communistic ticket, and was strongly opposed to his wife's registration with the party. MISS BURKE further stated that Subject had always voted Democratic tickets, and was heartily in favor of the policy of the New Deal.

MISS BURKE stated Subject is a very heavy drinker, but she had never seen him intoxicated. Subject's political philosophy, MISS BURKE considered to be merely "leftish" in the social changes calculated to improve the conditions of the working classes, and felt Subject's integrity to be unimpeachable.

AGENT'S NOTES:

Informant has the greatest respect for the literary work of Subject, but appeared to this Agent to be sincere and candid in her description of Subject's qualities.

CHARLES O. SHIELDS
Agent, CIC

CONFIDENTIAL

San Francisco, California
June 14, 1943
Case No. IX-O/S-14305c.

MEMORANDUM FOR THE OFFICER IN CHARGE

Subject: John E. Steinbeck
15041 Del Gado Drive
Sherman Oaks, California

Re: Residence check

On June 8, 1943, this Agent interviewed MR. HUGH PORTER, 344 California Street, San Francisco, California, purchaser of Subject's house in Los Gatos.

MR. PORTER did not know Subject personally, but had Subject's belongings moved from the house. He stated that Subject's second-class mail was tremendous, much of it apparently communistic. MR. PORTER read various parts at random and found it very radical. Subject's library, left in the former residence contained many radical books.

Informant's opinion of Subject based upon observation of conditions under which Subject lived is that Subject is very impulsive, eccentric, and unreliable socially. Informant had no knowledge of Subject's economical or political views except from the circumstantial evidence stated above.

MR. PORTER stated that Subject employed a Japanese house boy, Joe Nigahsi, who continued to work after Subject left. Nigahsi had books, ostensibly propaganda containing pictures of Axis leaders and accomplishments. Nigahsi is now evacuated to the interior.

Agent's notes: PORTER did not know Subject, but is very much opposed to economic and political views of Subject as indicated by type of mail received and contents of Subject's library.

CHARLES O. SHIELDS
Agent, CIC

CONFIDENTIAL

San Francisco, California
June 11, 1945
Case No. IX-O/S-14305c.

MEMORANDUM FOR THE OFFICER IN CHARGE

SUBJECT: JOHN E. STEINBECK

15041 Del Gado Drive
Sherman Oaks, California

Re: Check of Voter's Registration Files Santa Clara County, Calif.

On 9 June 1943 this Agent check the Voter's Registration files Santa Clara County, California to secure information concerning the Subject, who is being considered for a commission in the Army of the United States.

Registration files show that Subject's former wife, CAROL STEINBECK, registered as a Communist in Santa Clara County, 8 November 1938. On 16 September 1939, approximately one year later, Subject's wife registered in Santa Clara County as a Democrat. On the 13 June 1942, CAROL STEINBECK transferred her voting registration to Monterey, California.

No record was found of Subject having registered at any time as a Communist in Santa Clara County.

CHARLES O. SHIELDS
Agent, CIC

CONFIDENTIAL

San Francisco, California
June 11, 1945
Case No. IX-O/S-14305c.

MEMORANDUM FOR THE OFFICER IN CHARGE

SUBJECT: JOHN E. STEINBECK
15041 Del Gado Drive
Sherman Oaks, California

Re: Acquaintance check

On June 8, 1943, this Agent interviewed MR. K. L. ROBERTS, cashier First National Bank, Los Gatos, California.

Subject had an account in the bank from July 1, 1936 to June 26, 1941. Roberts impression of Subject was that he is very quiet and reserved. Subject usually is very poorly dressed.

Agent's notes: ROBERTS had no knowledge of Subject's economical or political views, and had not heard any derogatory remarks concerning his loyalty or integrity.

CHARLES O. SHIELDS
Agent, CIC

CONFIDENTIAL

San Francisco, California
30 June 1943
Case No. IX-O/S-14305c.

MEMORANDUM FOR THE OFFICER IN CHARGE

SUBJECT: JOHN E. STEINBECK
15041 Del Gado Drive
Sherman Oaks, California

Re: Residence Check.

On June 8, 1943, this Agent interviewed MR. F. RAINEORI, Los Gatos, California, neighbor of Subject, during the time Subject resided in Los Gatos.

Informant stated that Subject was friendly but generally very aloof. Subject, according to RAINEORI, apparently made frequent visits out of town while living in Los Gatos. RAINEORI recalled no derogatory remarks concerning Subject; however, informant had heard that Subject was very sensitive and desired to be avoided by the local people so that he could concentrate on his writing without interruption.

Agent's note: This neighbor lived approximately one-half mile from Subject and had little in common with Subject.

CHARLES O. SHIELDS
Agent, CIC

CONFIDENTIAL

San Francisco, California
30 June 1943
Case No. IX-O/S-14305c.

MEMORANDUM FOR THE OFFICER IN CHARGE

SUBJECT: JOHN E. STEINBECK
15041 Del Gado Drive
Sherman Oaks, California

Re: Interview with Mr. Martin Ray, Acquaintance.

On June 9, 1943, this Agent interviewed MR. MARTIN RAY, intimate acquaintance of Subject. Ray associated with STEINBECK and his former wife, CAROL STEINBECK, during the entire time Subject's residence was in Los Gatos, California. Informant is presently residing on Masson Road, Saratoga, California.

RAY believes Subject to be absolutely loyal to the government although Subject associated with some elements of the Communist Party in his earliest days of writing. Subject repeatedly stated to RAY that he was not a Communist but was interested in the lower-class working people regardless of their particular political creed. RAY explained that Subject had written certain articles for publications which were considered Communistic but that these articles were written to explain Subject" point of view of the social problem involved and not to further the interest of the Communist Party. Subject, according to RAY, gradually realised that he was being used by the Party and severed all connections with this element after his books began to have a wide sale.

CAROL STEINBECK, former wife of Subject, told RAY that she registered with the Communist Party in Santa Clara County in 1938 simply to observe the local reaction and that Subject was strongly opposed to this act.

Following the sale of one of Subject's earlier books, Subject and his wife made a trip to Europe, visiting Sweden and Russia. RAY stated that

Subject was deeply impressed by the economic and political policies of Sweden but was not impressed, nor did he discuss, the government of Russia.

Concerning Subject's character, RAY stated Subject's integrity was beyond question. Subject is very sensitive and sentimental; is deeply devoted to his friends and is easily influenced by these friends to grant large favors.

RAY believes subject should be commissioned in the Army only if Subject's writing ability may be efficiently utilised. According to RAY, Subject would work very hard writing for the benefit of his country but is not qualified to hold a commission in any other situation.

AGENT'S NOTES: RAY is a close friend of Subject and has tremendous respect for Subject's writing ability. This Agent believes Ray is interested in Subject's welfare as a friend yet was absolutely fair and impartial in his recollections of Subject and Subject's suitability for a commission in the Army.

CHARLES O. SHIELDS
Agent, CIC

CONFIDENTIAL

San Francisco, California
15 July 1943
Case No. IX-O/S-14305c.

MEMORANDUM FOR THE OFFICER IN CHARGE

SUBJECT: JOHN E. STEINBECK
15041 Del Gado Drive
Sherman Oaks, California

Re: Credit Check

On 13 July 1943 this Agent checked the records of the Retail Credit Association, 15 Stockton Street, San Francisco, California regarding the Subject. These records include reports from the Retail Merchant's Association of San Jose, California covering Santa Clara County.

The credit records indicate that the Subject enjoyed an excellent rating in 1940, had very good commercial and savings accounts in various California banks. Subject's income stated to be solely from writings and sale of stories to the motion picture industry.

CHARLES O. SHIELDS
Agent, CIC

WAR DEPARTMENT
MILITARY INTELLIGENCE DIVISION

By letter dated 16 February, 1943, from the (illegible) and Fourth Army, Presidio of San Francisco, California, to the (illegible) Office, (illegible), and Fourth Army, San Francisco, California, it was requested that a proper investigation be made in this area to determine the discretion, integrity and loyalty of Subject, and his suitability to hold a commission in the army

of the United States.
Details:

Fourteen-point (illegible) Outline: This (illegible) supplements previous record prepared at Los Angeles, California, under date of 27 January, 1943, made by Special Agent D.L. Johnson, CIC, Los Angeles, California.

Personal Data:
Birth: 27 January, 1902, Salinas, California
Present Age: 41 years
Description: Height 5' 11 1/3"; weight 207 lbs.
Characteristics: Loyal, honest, sincere, competent author, industrious, sensitive nature, (Names A,B,C,D,E,F,G,H)
Marital Status: Received interlocutory decree of divorce 12 March, 1943.

2. Family Data: Father, John Ernst Steinbeck (deceased), born in St. Augustine, Florida.
Mother, Olive Esther Steinbeck (deceased), born in Salinas, California.
Sister: Mrs. W.W. Bakker, Carmel, California.
Wife: Carol Steinbeck, interlocutory decree of divorce, 12 March, 1943

3. Education: 1915, Salinas Union School, graduated; 5 years at Leland Stanford University; majored in journalism; did not graduate.

4. Employment: At present working for

self as an author; had sold stories to the Motion Picture Industry.

March 1942 to December 1943, employed as Special Consultant to the Secretary of War, assigned to the Commanding General, Army Air Forces. Made an exhaustive study of flying and training, and now writing an official book on this subject. No salary.

December 1942 to March 1943, employed by the Office of War Information, 570 Madison Avenue, New York City, as a Foreign News editor at a salary of $3,000.00 per year.

Also Vice-President of the Pacific Biological Laboratories, Inc., for a number of years where he helped to operate a commercial laboratory.

5. Military History: None

6. Unit and Office Check: None

7. Addresses: 1942 to present, 15041 Del Gado Drive, Sherman Oakes, Calif.

December, 1941 to March, 1942, New York City, New York.

July, 1936 to December, 1941, Los Gatos, California.

Subject has lived most of his life near Salinas and Carmel, California, except for the time spent in Los Gatos and on intermittent trips to Los Angeles, New York City, and other parts of the world. (Names B, H)

8. Residence Check: Mr. Hugh Porter, 244 California Street, San Francisco California; pur-

chaser of Subject's former residence at Los Gatos. (U) Name B)

Mr. F. Rainari, neighbor of Subject at Los Gatos, California, (B) Name H)

9. Organisations:
   Western Writers' Congress, 1938
   Committee to Aid Agricultural
   Organisation, 1938. (Memo I)
   Schneiderman-Darcy Defense Committee, 1940 (Name L)
   Emergency Youth Assembly, 1937. (Name L)

International Union of Revolutionary Writers of Moscow.

League of American Writers, 19(illegible)

National Institute of Arts and Letters 19 (illegible)

10. Principal Amusements: Marine Biology.

11. References: No references given in San Francisco, California area.

12. Acquaintances: Mr. Martin Ray, Saratoga, Calif. (illegible)
    Miss Barbara Burke, 3055 Jackson Street, San Francisco, California (illegible)
    Mr. H.L. Roberts, Cashier, First National Bank, Los Gatos, California (illegible)
    Mr. Webster Street, of (illegible) Martin & Ferranis, California, (illegible)

Mrs. Carol Steinbeck, 425 Bradley Avenue, Pacific Grove, California (illegible)

13. Credit Record: Satisfactory. (name K).

14. Police Record: San Francisco Police Dept. (Name L)
Federal Bureau of Investigation, San Francisco (illegible) files refer to one, JOHN STEINBECK, PO Box 321, Los Gatos, Calif. as subscriber to PEOPLE'S WORLD, as of Sept. 1939 American Legion Radical Research Bureau, San Francisco, show record of Subject from November 9, 1935 through June 4, 1939. (Name L)
Sheriff's Office, Santa Clara County, Calif (illegible)
Los Gatos Police Dept. (illegible)
Salinas, California Police dept. (illegible)
Carmel Calif. Police Dept. (illegible)
Monterey Calif. Police dept. (illegible)

ADVERSE INFORMATION:

1. Subject has associated with individuals who are known to have a radical political and economic philosophy, and with members of the Communist party (Names A, B, C and H).

2. Subject received large volume of Communistic literature and possessed books expressing radical political and economic views in his library (illegible).

3. Subject's former wife, Carol Steinbeck, registered as a Communist in Santa Clara County in

1935 (names B, ... illegible)

UNDEVELOPED LEADS: Request investigations as follows:

A (C?) of (S?), G-2 2nd Service Command, Governors Island, New York

(1) Interview Subject's agents, McIntosh and Otis, 18 East 41st Street, New York City, to determine Subject's associations and activities in that vicinity. Such leads should be developed with particular attention to Communist associations and relations.

(2) To determine what relations has had with the League of American Writers by contacting the League's headquarters in New York City.

(3) To contact Major Betweiler, AAF, 25 Broad Street, New York City, who has made allegations that Subject is quite a heavy drinker and has communistic tendencies.

(4) Make an office and employment check at the offices of War Information, 570 Madison Avenue, New York City, where Subject was employed from December 1941 to March, 1945.

A C of S, MIS, War Department, Washington, D.C.

(1) To make necessary office and employment

check to determine Subject's employment as a Special Consultant to the Secretary of War, assigned to the Commanding General, Army Air Forces. Particular attention to be given to any possible Communist associations and connections.

(2) To check with FBI, OWI, MIS and Dies Committee files to determine any record extant on Subject. The Dies Committee should have a resume of Subject's activities written by Thomas Cavett for the Los Angeles Office of the Dies Committee.

REMARKS AND CONCLUSIONS:

This investigation revealed that Subject is honest, loyal, patriotic and an excellent and sincere writer. Although Subject exercised poor discretion during his early days of writing by associating with some elements of the Communist Party, he was not interested in advancing the cause of the Party but in gathering material for his writings on certain social conditions existing in this country at that time.

Subject wrote various articles which were published by Communist organizations because the economic views expressed were considered radical. However, Subject rejected communistic political and economic theories repeatedly and discarded his association with this element when it became apparent that his prestige was being used to further the interests of the Party.

Subject, in this Agent's opinion, possesses the requisites of honesty loyalty and discretion necessary for a commission in the Army of the United States. Subject is sincere in his beliefs concerning the social and economic situation of the under classes in this country and in his desire to have their lot improved.

Subject is a candid and powerful writer.

RECOMMENDATIONS:

This agent recommends that Subject be given a commission in the Army of the United States if he can be placed where his writing ability may be utilized.

G-2 NOTE:

This office does not concur in the recommendations of the investigative agent, and believing that substantial doubt exists as to Subject's loyalty and discretion, recommends that Subject not be favorably considered for a commission in the Army of the United States. Undeveloped leads will not be followed in the absence of a request, and this case is considered closed in this office.

APPROVED:

T. M. FAIRCHILD
LT. Colonel, MI
Officer in Charge

Subj previously disapproved
for a Commission by War Dept.
Personnel Board
WAH

27 July 1943
IX-O/S-14305c

Subject: John E. Steinbeck, 15041 De Gado Drive,
Sherman Oaks, California
To: Chief, MIS, War Department, Washington, D.C.

1. Attention is invited to our CI-R1 report dated 27 January 1943, Subject as above, representing investigation conducted in the vicinity of Los Angeles, California, and memorandum report dated 25 April 1943, Subject as above, covering investigation conducted in the Second Service Command previously forwarded your office.

2. Enclosed find CI-R1 report dated 13 July 1943 representing investigation conducted in the vicinity of San Francisco, California.

3. This office does not concur in the recommendations by the reporting agent in closing report. In view of substantial doubt as to Subject's loyalty and discretion, it is recommended that Subject not be considered favorably for a commission in the Army of the United States.

4. Undeveloped leads will not be followed in the absence of request, and this case is considered closed in this office.

For the AC of S, G-2:

TOP SECRET

BORIS T. PASH
Lt. Col., M.I.
Chief, Counter Intelligence Branch

Military, Intelligence Service
Washington
August 13, 1943

Subject: Letter of Transmittal.

To: Honorable J. Edgar Hoover,
Director, Federal Bureau of Investigation,
United States Department of Justice,
Washington, D.C.

The attached communications are forwarded for your information and such action as you consider available.

For the Chief, Military Intelligence Services

L. R. FORNEY
Colonel, General Staff Corps, Asst. Executive Officer, MIS.

The archives include the following memo written by a Birch D. O'Neal (date stamped March 27, 1944). The originating address was redacted, but since a Civil Attaché is part of a U.S. foreign embassy, the assumption can be made that this memo came from the U.S. Embassy in Mexico City, since Steinbeck traveled to Mexico. The last short paragraph was also redacted. No such "two copies" appear in the Steinbeck archives. But this is evidence that the FBI also followed the activities of Ernst Hemingway, which was widely known since Hemingway used his ship the Pilar on an anti-submarine patrols during World War Two, with the tacit approval of the U.S. Embassy in Havana.

Director, FBI

Re: John Steinbeck
Mexico Latin American Matters

Dear Sir:

There are enclosed for the Bureau's information two copies of a memorandum for the Ambassador dated March 22, 1944, containing information relative to this individual and to Ernst Hemingway, well-known writer.
(Redacted)

Very truly yours,

Birch D. O'Neal
Civil Attaché

The FBI continues to follow Steinbeck out of and back into the country. On April 8, 1944, the SAC (Special Agent in Charge, or bureau chief) of the San Antonio FBI office forwards a memorandum of Steinbeck's reentry into the U.S. via Brownsville, Texas, from Mexico. The FBI office in San Antonio also forwards the same memo to the New York City office of the FBI.

CONFIDENTIAL

April 8, 1944

To: Director, FBI

From: SAC, San Antonio

Subject: John Ernst Steinbeck
Incoming Passenger, Brownsville, Texas
3/15/44
Foreign Travel Control

Reference is made to Bureau memorandum to San Antonio dated March 21, 1944, in the above-captioned matter. For the information of the New York City Office, reference memorandum advised that an investigation was conducted by Military Intelligence Division concerning the above-captioned individual to determine his loyalty and suitability to hold a commission in the Army of the United States, and that information had been received by the Bureau indicating that in view of substantial doubt as to the loyalty and discretion of the subject, a recommendation was made that he should not be considered favorably for a Commission in the U.S. Army.

This is to advise that on March 15, 1944, the subject, accompanied by his wife, GWYN CONGER STEINBECK, entered Brownsville, Texas, via Pan

American Clipper enroute from the Reforma Hotel, Mexico, D. F. to their residence at 330 E. 51st Street, New York City. At the time of their entry, it was ascertained that the subject was an American citizen born at Salinas, California, on February 27, 1902, and that his wife was also an American citizen, having been born in Chicago, Illinois, October 25, 1916. It was also learned that the subject is presently employed as a writer by the *New York Herald Tribune* and that in 1943 he had been on a six-months assignment to England, Africa, and Sicily as a war correspondent.

The subject advised that on that assignment he had been slightly wounded and that the purpose of his present two-months trip to Mexico City had been to regain his health before resuming is work for the above-mentioned newspaper.

The above is being submitted for the information of the Bureau and a copy of this letter has been designated for the information of the New York City Office. No further action in this matter is presently contemplated by this Office.

The FBI files contain a brief clipping from page 2 of the U.S. Communist paper, the *Daily Worker*, about Steinbeck's appearance at an international forum sponsored by the newspaper, *The New York Herald Tribune*. Photographer Robert Capa also appeared, as he had accompanied Steinbeck's throughout the Soviet Union for the *Herald Tribune*. Steinbeck's reportage was published as the book *A Russian Journal* in 1948, but events changed the Soviet Union so rapidly after World War Two that Steinbeck's book was largely out-of-date when it was first published. It is now one of his least republished works.

The page from the Steinbeck archives carries these notations at the bottom right corner of the page:

> This is a clipping from
> Page 2 of the
> Daily Worker
> Date 10-24-47
> Clipped at the Seat of
> Government

Does the annotation ("Seat of the Government") mean Washington, D.C.?

Found Soviets Eager for Peace, Capa, Steinbeck Tell Trib Forum

The word most frequently heard during their recent tour of the Soviet Union was "peace," author John Steinbeck and photographer Robert Capa told the fourth session of the Herald Tribune Forum Wednesday evening.

Capa read a joint report of their observations while visiting the Ukraine, Georgia and Great Russian industrial cities as a self-styled "cold war team" of correspondents.

"These people were destroyed and hurt much more than any that I have seen during my ten years of battlefields and they hate war more than any one I ever talked to," declared Capa.

He said a halt of the "vicious and insane game" of recriminations between Russia and the U.S. would find immediate approval among Russian masses. He stated Russians were particularly interested in hearing about "the persecution of liberals" in America and that he and Steinbeck told them "to our knowledge there are no political prisoners in the United States yet."

"I am holding my fingers crossed," he told the Forum audience. . . . "We do not know who started this vicious and insane game of stupid accusation and violent criticism. It is not very important who started it. The important thing is who is going to stop it.

"The people of Russia in our little experience want the same things our people do — food, shelter, security and the ability to raise and feed and educate their children in peace. And this is the really important thing. That is all."

Without any annotation, two newspaper articles, containing two chapters from *A Russian Journal,* appears in the FBI archives. They appear to have been published in *The New York Herald Tribune,* as Steinbeck's research tour of the Soviet Union was sponsored by *The Herald Tribune.* These articles may have been published in *The San Francisco Examiner,* as it is mentioned in a preface to one article.

It is relatively unusual for clippings to appear without any sort of annotation, regarding their dates or value to the FBI.

These pages appear in the Appendix.

The FBI files also contain another protest letter about Steinbeck, from an anonymous citizen, writing from San Simeon, California. The writer's name has been redacted. The entire letter appears in the Appendix.

Jan. 18, 1947

Hon. J. Edgar Hoover
Washington, D.C.

Dear Sir:

I trust that your agents in San Francisco are watching these series of articles with much interest.

No doubt you have a file on this John Steinbeck; one of our foremost Commie inspired writers who had written many stories whose theme was to stir up class consciousness. Grapes of Wrath etc.

The most shocking element here is the fact that Steinbeck is even given space on the San Francisco, after being denounced by W. R, Hearst back in 38 or 39. As you know doubt know, [REDACTED] blasted this picture Grapes of Wrath, seeing the underlying motives.

The very same executives on this paper purged this girl for her (illegible — may be constant) Attack on the Commie themes emanating from Hollywood.

I wrote a letter to [REDACTED] of the Los Angeles Examiner, regarding this Steinbeck, seeking to hold up the articles. Also asking just who was responsible for this right about face. It seems that this is the only nearest sheet that is carring Steinbeck's series.

How can Steinbeck have such "easy access to "INSIDE THE IRON CURTAIN" when YOU and other LOYAL Americans are forbidden to enter. San Francisco is a veritable LITTLE MOSCOW to be sure.

I fully realize that the Examiner came out "finally" for the new Local Mayor Robinson, who ran on an Anti Commie platform. But the paper finally entered picture after Robinson had a commanding lead. "(illegible) stating that they were Robinson because they figured he would win" . . . NOT because he was the best man mind you or the principles that he stood for . . .

When I arrived here a year ago, I proceeded to inform Robinson of Frank Havenner's record in Washington, which had been kept very much in the dark on the West Coast. With all this information it was clear sailing to be sure. This RED minority element in San Francisco is plenty dangerous, and a verit powder keg. Of course I appreciate the fact that I am not telling you any thing that is new.

This Steinbeck running in the Examiner over Ada's dead body, a girl who was willing to sacrifice her very life for her country stands vindicated today for the fight she had even within her own ranks on this paper. I expected [REDACTED] to bring this matter to Mr. Hearst's attention, who is residing as you know, in Beverly Hills.

I trust that this information will prove to be helpful to you.

With kindest regards,

Yours most/sincerely,

[REDACTED]

San Simeon, Calif.

J. Edgar Hoover replies to the California writer: Hoover also replied to such complaint letters about the activities of Elvis Presley, although in the case of Presley he at least once replied with the admonition that he was not the guardian of the nation's morality, an image that he himself had nurtured for years. (See: *The FBI Files on Elvis Presley*, passim.)

This memo has to be read from the bottom

section up: an anonymous FBI employee wrote the bottom: NOTE: section as advice and a prompt to Hoover.

J. Edgar Hoover was then able to reply accurately to the citizen complaint, in the top section, which was then mailed to the citizen.

January 26, 1948

[REDACTED]
San Simeon, California

Dear [REDACTED]

Your letter dated January 18, 1948, with enclosures, has been received, and I want to express my appreciation to you for having brought this matter to my attention.

Sincerely yours,

John Edgar Hoover
Director

NOTE: This individual has corresponded with the Bureau on several previous occasions on matters of similar nature, and now draws the Director's attention to John Steinbeck as a Communist in connection with a series of articles Steinbeck wrote concerning Russia.

The FBI files also contains a clipping of a

review of *A Russian Journal*, which appeared in *The Daily Worker*, April 16, 1948.

The page also contains the notations:

This is a clipping from
Page 12 of the
Daily Worker

Date 4-16-48
Clipped at the Seat of
Government.

(Steinbeck's *A Russian Journal* never satisfied Communist critics such as *The Daily Worker* nor was it critically well-received in the U.S. mainstream press.)

Book Parade

John Steinbeck's A Russian Journal

BY ROBERT FRIEDMAN

John Steinbeck's warm sympathy for people, as evidenced in his A Russian Journal, (published today) is the one positive feature of an account of a visit to the Soviet Union which is otherwise overrun with frivolous provincialism and a coy disinclination to face political realities.

Steinbeck has taken out the conventional insurance against criticism by concluding that his journal "will not be satisfactory either to the ecclesiastical Left nor the Lumpen Right. The first will say it is anti-Russian, and the second that it is pro-Russian. Surely it is superficial, and how could it be otherwise? We have no conclusions to draw, except that Russian people are like all other people in the world. Some bad ones there are surely, but by far the greater number are very good."

Now the above is pretty childish stuff. It is a fraudulent 'objectivity' which presumes to be accurate merely because it is inconsistent and superficial enough to draw fire from all sides. And it was a waste of Mr. Steinbeck's time to discover so laboriously that all people are alike.

What a reader logically expects from a "Russian journal" is not a platitude but an examination of the way of life of a people which right now is definitely not like that of "all other people."

* * *

THIS STEINBECK HAS NOT done, even to the minimum extent required (illegible) impressions as (illegible) as say, to a more thorough study. This reviewer frankly could not decide whether Steinbeck's failure was due to choice or to an appalling political illiteracy.

What is one to say of a writer to whom the distinctive characteristic of American capitalist society is that it provides a government of "checks and balances?" Or of the naivete which has it that "our government is designed to keep anyone from getting too much power or, having got it, from keeping it"? And, "we agreed," Steinbeck writes solemnly, "that this makes our country function more slowly, but that it certainly makes it function more surely."

It is foolhardly for a man who does not know the facts of life in his own backyard to fare forth as an interpreter of his neighbor.

There is little in A Russian Journal to indicate that Steinbeck has any comprehension of Marxism, the cause for war, the fundamental difference between capitalism and socialism. He doesn't like war and he says so. He would hate to see another one. He is fond of children and good, honest people, Russian as well as any other kind.

But his Journal is filled

with trivia which will not help people understand the first socialist state because Steinbeck himself never bothered to find out.

* * *

HE IS PROVINDIAL, in a petty way, complaining that Russians always think they have discovered or invented products or methods which Steinbeck points out, they really didn't. This, from a native of a l and in which U.S. contest winners of all kinds are automatically described as unquestioned world's champions.

He writes feelingly of the reverence throughout the world for the memory of Roosevelt. Yet he complains of a like tribute by the Soviet peoples to Stalin and sneeringly intimates that Stalin was a hypocrite in objecting to adulation.

Steinbeck makes the conventional bourgeois plaint about Soviet censorship and "suspicion" of foreigners and cutely explains them as traditional Russian behaviour. Very possibly and, in the light of the author's political maturity this is not sarcastic – Steinbeck does not know of the 30-year effort through conspiracy and armed attack by capitalist states to destroy the Soviet Union.

One could go on quoting Steinbeck, but what for? A Russian Journal is much more enlightening about the kind of culture which develops such intellectual Sad (illegible) than about the Soviet Union.

Robert Capa's photographs, which illustrate the text are striking and excellently reproduced.

This is a clipping from Page 12 of the Daily Worker

Date 4-16-48
Clipped at the
Seat of Government.

Also as if to balance their criticism, the FBI files also contains a clipping of a review of *A Russian Journal,* which appeared in *The New Leader.*

The front page of a two-page clipping, also contains the notations:

> This is a clipping from
> Page 11 of the
> New Leader
>
> Date 8-21-48
> Clipped at the Seat of
> Government.

Steinbeck Sans Wrath

REVIEWED BY ALLAN DANE

A Russian Journal. By John Steinbeck, with pictures by Robert Capa.
New York: Viking Press. 220 pages. $3.75

Mr. Steinbeck has joined the fraternity of vodka visitors. For three weeks he toured the Soviet Union under the subtle guidance of VOKS, the government agency for "cultural liason," saw Moscow celebrate its 800th anniversary, got stomach cramps from overeating on a collective farm, inspected the ruins of Stalingrad, was wined and dined in Georgia, flew back to Moscow, where he chattered with American officials and correspondents, came home and wrote a book.

Now Mr. Steinbeck did see a few things that may prove interesting to the average reader, and Robert Capa contributes a few nice (but not exceptional) shots of life in Russia. There are impressive descriptions of wartime destruction, of the shortage of artificial limbs, of Soviet inefficiency and "snafu." Steinbeck give some curious examples of black market activities in Russia, of transportation difficulties, of the sickening hero-worship of the leaders.

The careful reader will be able to detect a few other interesting bits of information: the survival of deep religious feeling in the country; the greater emphasis on government building rather than on residential housing construction; the utter lack of humor and the depressing serenity of Moscow, as contrasted wit the climate of greater spontaneity as one gets further away from the bureaucratic center.

And yet, one cannot help questioning Mr. Steinbeck's understanding of Russia. He went to Moscow as an "honest and liberal" man, he says, not to concern himself with "politics and the larger issues" but "simply to report . . . neither critically nor favorably." But how can he speak of life in a totalitarian state without constantly referring to the government and its agencies? How sure is he that he got to the "people" and not merely to a model farm in the Ukraine and to a show-case sanatorium on the Black Sea? If Mr. Steinbeck was merely after the answers to such questions as "Do children go to school in Russia?" He could have saved himself the trouble of going. He speaks no Russian, and all his contact was made through official interpreters. Steinbeck, whom the Russians consider one of America's top figures, was wined and dined, was taken to a Moscow nightclub and to a Kiev cocktail bar, went to the country home of such Soviet millionaires as Alexander Korneichuk — and concludes that the Russians have plenty to eat; he even states that the quality of Russian clothing improved during the few weeks he spent in Russia.

* * *

HE ATTENDED the celebration of the 800th anniversary of Moscow with Louis Aragon, the French Stalinist writer, and was impressed by the splendor of festivities. Capa gets led around Moscow by a special official assigned "to facilitate his movements about the city"; "in Red Square he had a militia man assigned to him to make things easy and stop any unpleasantness"; yet throughout the book Steinbeck never mentioned the MVD.

Most startling, perhaps, is Steinbeck's own attitude toward the Soviet Union. His book is full of what Koestler would call false equations. When Capa is stopped from taking pictures at a lend-leased tractor plant in Stalingrad, Steinbeck reminds us that foreigners may not photograph Oak Ridge either. In his mind, "Moscowitis" and "Washingtonitis" cancel each other out. When he admits that the collective farm he was shown put on a big show for him, he insists that "any Kansas farmer" would do the same for his guests.

Steinbeck wants "peace" and hates all "curtains," iron or otherwise. He does not care about governments, good or bad. He comes up with a conclusion that is neither here nor there: "We knew nothing about the things American papers were howling about — Russian military preparations, atomic research, slave labor, the political skullduggery of the Kremlin." And he still doesn't. As a matter of fact, he is proud of his ignorance. Even Capa is led to remark that "Steinbeck is so goddamn innocent that all questions posed by the curious and hero-worshipping Russian population are answered by a friendly grunt, 'This I do not know.'" When he is asked if the American people want war with Russia, he replies: "We don't know." Whether the question concerns Wallace's popularity or American foreign policy, the agnosticism and decadence of American (illegible) or U.S. support of reactionaries and fascists, Steinbeck's answer is invariably, "I don't now . . . no one tells us these things."

Under such circumstances it is not surprising that the world-shaking conclusion to Steinbeck's conducted tour is that "the Russian people are people," "that they are very nice." He adds that they want "the same things all people want – good lives, increased comfort, security, and peace." But he does not tell us if the Russian people are getting any of these.

* * *

STEINBECK USED TO BE known as a man with a strong social conscience. *The Grapes of Wrath* and *Tortilla Flat* were full of righteous moral indignation about social and economic injustice. In *The Moon is Down* Steinbeck made a heated if somewhat pedestrian attack on totalitarian aggression and conquest. Those were the days when Steinbeck could be counted upon to stand up and wield his pen in behalf of democracy and freedom. Even today had he gone to Spain or china, he would surely not have come back to write a book in order to demonstrate that the "Chinese people want good lives and comfort or that "the Spaniards like peace."

This is a clipping from
Page 11 of the
New Leader
Date 8-21-48
Clipped at the seat of
Government.

The following fact sheet was on file in 1952; the Bureau states "The FBI has not conducted an investigation on this individual." A request for this information may have come from the State Department, as the fact sheet carries the annotation, at the bottom left, "Original to State Department."

March 18, 1952

John Ernst Steinbeck

Reference is made to your request for information subsequent to February 13, 1948, concerning John Ernst Steinbeck, the writer. The FBI has not conducted an investigation on this individual.

A review of the files however, revealed newspaper reviews from the "Daily Worker" dated April 16, 1948, and the "New Leader" dated August 21, 1948, of John Steinbeck's book, "A Russian Journal". This book was published in April, 1948, by the Viking Press in new York and contained pictures by Robert Capa. The publication was based on experiences which the two "self-styled cold war team" had on a three weeks visit to Soviet Russia during the summer of 1947.

The writers of the reviews both seemed to doubt Mr. Steinbeck's ability to portray life in Soviet Russia authoritatively since he was there for such a short period of time.

The foregoing information is furnished to you

as a result of a request for an FBI file check only and is not to be considered as a clearance or non-clearance of the individual involved. It is for your confidential use only and is not to be disseminated outside of your agency.

Original to State Department

On March 1, 1954, the Bureau sent a one-page fact sheet on Steinbeck to the United States Information Agency (U.S.I.A.), in response to a request for information by the U.S.I.A. This fact sheet or memorandum carries the annotation at the bottom left: Original to USIA. Request received 1/31/54

SECRET

March 1, 1954

John Steinbeck
Born: February 27, 1902
Salinas, California

No investigation has been conducted by this Bureau concerning the above-named individual. A review of the files, however, reflects that in May, 1945, a reliable source advised that the American Youth for Democracy in a list captioned "Recommended Reading List for American Youth for Democracy," listed the book entitled "The Moon is Down" by John Steinbeck. The American Youth for Democracy has been designated by the

Attorney General of the United States pursuant to Executive Order 10450. (2 lines redacted)

Another Government agency, who conducts investigations abroad, advised that on August 23, 1947, a correspondent of the "Daily Worker," an East coast Communist publication, was in Rio De Janeiro, Brazil, conferring with leaders of the Communist Party in Brazil. The discussion related to invitations to visit Brazil to be sent to various American writers and to ascertain whether they would be permitted to remain in Rio De Janeiro. The name of John Steinbeck was given as one who would receive an invitation from the Communist Party in Brazil.

The files further reflect that newspaper reviews appeared in the April 16, 1948, issue of the "Daily Worker," and the August 21, 1948, issue of the "New Leader" concerning John Steinbeck's book, "A Russian Journal" relating to his experiences while on a three week tour of the Soviet Union in the summer of 1947. The writers of the reviews appeared to doubt Steinbeck's ability to portray life in Soviet Russia authoritatively since he was there for such a short period of time.

In the reports of the Special Committee on Un-American Activities, Seventy-Eighth Congress, Second Session, House Report No. 1311 on page 101 it is pointed out that "the National Maritime Union of America has toed the Communist Party line through all its changes in recent years. The ships of the American Merchant Marines are being supplied with libraries for the seamen to read while at sea and the National Maritime

Union's educational department is responsible for the selection of the books. John Steinbeck's 'Grapes of Wrath' is naturally present, as it would be in any Communist's selection."

The foregoing information is furnished to you as a result of your request for an FBI file check only and is not to be construed as a clearance or a nonclearance of the individual involved. This information is furnished for your use and should not be disseminated outside of your agency.

Original to USIA.

The longest and most detailed summary on Steinbeck appeared dated March 10, 1954 and consists of nearly eight single-spaced pages of Italic type, divided into these seven sections:

BIOGRAPHICAL DATA:
BUREAU INVESTIGATION:
INVESTIGATION BY G-2:
AFFILIATION WITH COMMUNIST FRONT ORGANIZATIONS
INSTANCES WHEREIN AMERICA'S ENEMIES HAVE USED OR ATTEMPTED TO USE STEINBECK'S WRITINGS AND REPUTATION TO FURTHER THEIR CAUSES:
ASSOCIATION WITH COMMUNIST PARTY MEMBERS AND CONTROVERSY WITH COMMUNIST PARTY:
MISCELLANEOUS:

Many of the paragraphs contain references to

the sources of information, either by government document reference number or by general annotation. The second and third paragraphs in the section INVESTIGATION BY G-2 beginning: "Steinbeck was investigated by G-2 during 1942 so as to determine his suitability to hold a commission in the U.S. Army," carry the annotation "per Army" at the end of each paragraph.

These pages appear in full in the Appendix.

March 10, 1954

John Ernst Steinbeck

Biographical Data:

<u>BIOGRAPHICAL DATA:</u>

John Ernst Steinbeck, author, playwright and war correspondent, was born at Salinas, California, on February 27, 1902. He graduated from Salinas High School in 1918 and was a student at Stanford University for five years but did not graduate. He married Carol Henning in 1930 and was divorced from her in March, 1943. He married Gwyn Conger on March 29, 1943, and Elaine Scott on December 28, 1950. He has been the author of a number of books and was awarded the Pulitzer prize in 1940. Among the books for which he is most noted are "Tortilla Flat," 1935; "Of Mice And Men," 1937; "Grapes Of Wrath," 1939; "The Moon Is Down," 1942; "Cannery Row," 1945; "The Wayward Bus," 1947; and "A Russian Journal," 1948. He was also employed as a war correspondent and as a writer for the "New York Herald Tribune" during 1943, 1944, 1947, and 1948. Steinbeck was Vice President of World Video, Inc., an organization chartered in New York State on December 18, 1947, for the purpose of preparing television programs. ("Who's Who In America," 1942-100-166188-2; [part sentence redacted] 100-340922-111, p. 1, 9 43)

BUREAU INVESTIGATION:

The Bureau has conducted no investigation concerning John Steinbeck. However, under date of May 11, 1942, Attorney General Biddle forwarded to the Bureau a letter received by him from Steinbeck which stated in part "Do you suppose you could ask Edgar's boys to stop stepping on my heels? They think I am an enemy alien. It's getting tiresome." After checking the Bureau files the Attorney General was advised that Steinbeck was not being and never had been investigated. (100-106244-1)

INVESTIGATION BY G-2:

Steinbeck was investigated by G-2 during 1943 to determine his suitability to hold a commission in the U.S. Army. After investigation the Chief, Counter Intelligence Branch, G-2, recommended he not be considered favorably for a commission. Investigation developed that Steinbeck's former wife, Carol, had registered as a Communist in Santa Clara County, California, on November 6, 1938, but registered as a Democrat in 1939. According to Carol, she registered as a

Communist to see what would happen and to see what the reaction would be in a small town, but regretted this move because it reflected unfavorably on her husband. She and others advised that Steinbeck was a registered Democrat and probably favored the News Deal but he had never been a Communist.

This investigation also revealed that Steinbeck contributed articles to the November 9, 1936, and April 1, 1938, issues of "Pacific Weekly," cited as a Communist publication by the California Committee on Un-American Activities. He also subscribed to the "Daily People's World," west coast Communist newspaper, as of September 1939.

Associates and friends of Steinbeck advised G-2 that he was honest, loyal, patriotic, and an excellent and sincere writer. They stated that although he exercised poor discretion during is early days of writing by associating with some elements of the Communist Party, he was not interested in advancing the cause of the Party but in gathering material for his writings on certain social conditions existing in the United States at that time. They reported that he wrote various articles which were published by Communist organizations because the economic views expressed were considered radical. However, he rejected Communistic political and economical theories repeatedly and discarded his association with that element when it became apparent that his prestige was being used to further interests of the party.

AFFILIATION WITH COMMUNIST FRONT ORGANIZATIONS:

During 1938, Steinbeck granted the Simon J. Lubin Society of California, Inc., permission to republish his pamphlet entitled "Their Blood Is Strong," a story of the migratory agricultural workers in California, which was originally published in 1936. According to the California Committee on Un-American Activities, the Simon J. Lubin Society, Inc., was a Communist front for California agrarian penetration, organized in the Fall of 1936 by Unit 104 of the Professional Section of the Communist Party. (61-7559-2-999)

In approximately1938, the Committee to Aid Agricultural Workers was organized under Steinbeck's leadership. Steinbeck also served as chairman of this organization which has been referred to as the John Steinbeck Committee to Aid Agricultural Workers. According to one source of unknown reliability, this committee was organized after Steinbeck had exposed the situation of the migrant farmers and "Okies" in his books. This source stated there was nothing political in the work of the committee, the purpose being to gather food and clothing for those in need. Another source indicated that the committee furnished financial assistance to the United Cannery, Agricultural, Packing and Allied Workers of America. Many of the supporters of this organization were known to be Communist Party members or people who had been active in behalf of Communist united front organizations. The American Legion Radical Research Bureau described this committee as a "very Red outfit."

[Part of sentence REDACTED] Los Angeles [REDACTED] of the committee; [REDACTED] 100-166188-2; 100-339317-1; 100-6633-2, p. 104; 100-3-23-16, p. 12)

John Steinbeck was one of the sponsors and delegates to the Western Writers Congress (declared to be a subsidiary of the American Writers Congress, cited by the HCUA) conference held in San Francisco, California, on November 13 and 14, 1936. (Dies Committee hearing, Volume 3, Page 1996)

Steinbeck was active in the League of American Writers (cited by the Attorney General) during 1938-1940, serving that organization as one of the vice presidents in 1939 and as one of the board of directors of the California league of American Writers in 1940. He also furnished that organization with a statement for publication in a booklet published during May, 1938, and signed an open letter to all Senators and members of the House of Representatives during 1939. (61-7759-667812; 100-7322-8; 16; 61-7551-183110; 61-7561-2-87)

Steinbeck was among those who signed an open letter to the Government and People of the United States sponsored by the Washington Committee to Lift the Spanish Embargo (cited as a Communist front by the California Committee on Un-American Activities) on January 31, 1939. ("New York Times;" 121-23278-267112, p. 1506)

As of late 1940 or early 1941 the name of John Steinbeck was contained in the active indices of the National Federation For Constitutional Liberties (cited by the Attorney

General). (Anonymous; 100-1170-49, p. 157)

A clipping from the "New York Times" of February 21, 1945, reported the formation in New York City of a new cooperative publishing concern, namely, Associated Magazine Contributors, Inc. The initial list of owner-contributors included John Steinbeck. Associated Magazine Contributors was cited by the California Committee on Un-American Activities when it reported that ""he Communist influence is established through such news services." (123-11674-13)

In preparation for a reception to be given at the Waldorf-Astoria, New York City, on May 5, 1946, by the National Council of American-Soviet Friendship (NCAST — cited by the Attorney General) for three visiting Soviet literary figures, the Assistant to the Executive Director of the NCASF contacted Howard Fast, a well-known author and probable member the Cultural Section of the Communist Party in New York City, for his approval of a list of distinguished writers, publishers, artists, and other personalities to be invited to the affair. Fast declared that naturally anti-Soviets and Trotskyites should not be invited as they would make things "very uncomfortable." According to the informant the names of John Steinbeck was among those read off to Fast which met with his approval. ([REDACTED 100-14964-736)

On May 17, 1946, Mrs. Mariel Draper of New York, the Chairman of the Women's Section of the American NCASF, spoke at a meeting of the Democratic Women's International Federation in

Rome, Italy. In her speech she heartily agreed with the Soviet representative who had attacked United States foreign policy and reported that the American people were being given a dose of anti-Soviet propaganda worse than that against Germany before the Second World War. She stated that a number of individuals, including Steinbeck, had recently been converted to "the carp of war and anti-Sovietism." (5-18-48, "New York Herald Tribune;" 100-344442-A)

Bureau files reflect a number of instances from 1945 through 1950 wherein Steinbeck was approached by various other Communist Party front organizations to support their causes so as to enlist the widest possible mass support for their campaigns. There is no indication that he complied with these particular requests. (100-7061-923, p. 19; 100-334436-1521; 100-185087-7712; 100-370500-48)

INSTANCES WHEREIN AMERICA'S ENEMIES HAVE USED OR ATTEMPTED TO USE STEINBECK'S WRITINGS AND REPUTATION TO FURTHER THEIR CAUSES:

Bureau files reflect that because many of Steinbeck's writings portrayed an extremely sordid and poverty-stricken side of American life, they were reprinted in both German and Russian and used by the Nazis and Soviets as propaganda against America. (Numerous references)

An individual who had been employed during 1937 as a playwright on the Federal Theater Project, Works Progress Administration, testified before the Dies Committee that the Party told her what to write and furnished her with research material obtained from the Simon Lubin Society (previously cited). She advised that this material included some of Steinbeck's field notes in his handwriting, for his book "Grapes Of Wrath." (Testimony, Rena Vale on 7-22-40; Dies Committee Executive Hearings, Volume 3, Page 1219)

Steinbeck's book, "Grapes Of Wrath," was among the periodicals and books sold from the literature table at a Communist Party May Day meeting held on May 1, 1940, in Los Angeles, California. [REDACTED 61-7559-7883, p. 70)

A booklet announcing the courses of the Workers School of New York City, official Communist Party school, from the winter term, 1943, stated that the works of leading dramatic writers, including Steinbeck, would be used in the discussions of history of social institutions as they had been reflected by writers of all times. (1946 Report, California Committee on Un-American Activities; 100-15252-39, p. 440)

During March, 1945, a copy of a recommended reading list used by the American Youth For Democracy (cited by the Attorney General) indicated that listed books were available from the New Jersey State office of that organization at a discount. This list included Steinbeck's "The Moon Is Down." ([REDACTED] state headquarters of the Communist Political Association, Newark, New Jersey; 61-777-31-60, p. 24)

<u>ASSOCIATION WITH COMMUNIST PARTY MEMBERS AND CONTROVERSY WITH COMMUNIST PARTY</u>:

On June 2, 1953, an admitted former Communist Party member (about 1937-1939) testified before the House Committee on Un-American Activities that although Steinbeck had done more through his novel about the agricultural workers then anyone else for the Communist Party cause he appeared to be at odds with the Communist Party during that period although the witness could not state just how. (Roland William Kibbee, Executive Session testimony since publicly released; 51-7582-1975, p. 2330)

In letters written by San Darcy to Ella Winter (both Communist Party functionaries in California) during March, 1937, and November, 1940, Darcy indicated that Winter was well acquainted with Steinbeck and might have considerable influence with him. On March 7, 1937, he wrote "Needless to say, I am glad to hear about Steinbeck's new book. I hope it fulfills what you say. There is no reason why it should act. He can write, and, with the education I am told you and our friends have been giving him he ought to make the grade better than he did in his earlier book." Another undated letter obtained early in 1944 from Winter to Steinbeck indicated that Steinbeck had previously criticized Winter. This letter which was partially obscene attacked Steinbeck and indicated that he and Winter wee at odds. (Highly confidential sources; 100-18610-56, p. 23, 38, 77)

On June 23, 1950, Louis Budenz, former Managing Editor of the "Daily Worker," east coast Communist newspaper, and an admitted former

Communist Party member, advised as follows: "Carey McWilliams is a writer, particularly noted as the author of 'Factories In The Field,' published in 1939, which was the foundation of John Steinbeck's 'Grapes Of Wrath.' When this book was published, I was advised by Alexander Trachtenberg and Jack Stachel (both Communist Party functionaries) that McWilliams was under Communist discipline. His had a great deal to do with the way we handled this book and also John Steinbeck's book because at that time McWilliams was supposedly making a Communist of Steinbeck." (Interview with Budenz; 100-998-92)

[THREE FULL PARAGRAPHS REDACTED]

The June 11, 1948, issue of the Los Angeles "Examiner" stated that Ring Lardner, Jr., a screen writer, had signed with Steinbeck and others to write a film version of Steinbeck's story "Pastures Of Heaven." According to the "Examiner," this "was the first Hollywood employment given any of the 'unfriendly ten' since their refusal to answer the Communist question in Washington last fall" and the move challenged the Motion Picture Association of America's announcement that none of the men cited by Congress could work until cleared of the charge. (100-295885-11, p. 5)

MISCELLANEOUS:

From time to time communists for the "Daily Worker" and "Daily People's World" have criticized Steinbeck's writings and not portraying adequately the American Communists or supporting the American Communist movement. On the other hand these papers have also praised the books, stating in January, 1943, that he was one of the most popular authors among the Soviet Russians. Both Communists and anti-Communists criticized his 1946 series of articles for the "New York Herald Tribune" entitled "A Russian Journal," which he wrote after a visit to Russia in the Summer of 1947, as being too pro-Communist and too anti-Communist. Both sides criticized his ability to adequately portray life in Soviet Russia after such a short visit. It is noted that the articles criticized Soviet red tape and the Soviet Government but were favorable to the Russian people. (100-106224-A; 64-175-240-A; and others)

During 1942, 1943, and 1944, Steinbeck was listed as one of the individuals in the United States who received Russian literature. (Office of Censorship; 65-1674-809, p. 8; 65-49085-81)

On February 23, 1944, the Steinbecks attended a reception at the Russian Embassy in Mexico City. That reception celebrated the 26th anniversary of the founding of the Russian Army. ("Koveades," morning newspaper, 2/7/44; 100-145364-17)

On August 23, 1947, Joseph Starobin, correspondent of the "Daily Worker," was in Rio de Janeiro, Brazil, conferring with leaders of the Communist Party of Brazil regarding the possibility of inviting well-known American writers to Brazil. One of the Americans recommended by Starobin was Steinbeck. There is no information available indicating Steinbeck was actually invited. ([REDACTED] 100-51287-75, 81)

A Counter Intelligence Corps report of January 13, 1954, reported that there was a strong indication that the "Verlas der Nation," a publishing firm of the National Lemokratische Partei (a Soviet zone political party which had been described by G-2 as "presumably a conservative party" but which is an East Zone political party and as such is Communist oriented) was about to negotiate publishing rights with seven American authors, including Steinbeck. (A usually reliable source of CIC; 105-26240-1)

In late October, 1956, the Bureau sends a two-page summary about Steinbeck to an unnamed recipient. If this went out of the country, the notation "Orig. and one to CG" may mean Counsel General.

October 31, 1956
John Steinbeck
Born: February 27, 1902
Salinas, California

No investigation pertinent to your inquiry has been conducted by the FBI concerning the captioned individual. However, a review of FBI files reflects that in May, 1945, a source that has furnished reliable information in the past advised that the American Youth for Democracy in a list captioned "Recommended Reading List for American Youth for Democracy," listed the book entitled "The Moon Is Down" by John Steinbeck.

The American Youth for Democracy has been cited by the Attorney General pursuant to Executive Order 10450. (61-777-31-60 informant [REDACTED])

Another government agency which conducts investigations abroad advised that on August 23, 1947, a correspondent of the "Daily Worker," an east coast communist newspaper, was in Rio De Janeiro, Brazil, conferring with leaders of the Communist Party in Brazil. The discussion related to invitations to visit Brazil to be sent to various American writers and to ascertain whether they would be permitted to remain in Rio De Janeiro. The name of John Steinbeck was given as one who would receive an invitation from the Communist Party in Brazil. (100-51287-81)

The files further reflect that a newspaper review appeared in the April 16, 1948, issue of the "Daily Worker," concerning John Steinbeck's book, "A Russian Journal," relating to his experiences while on a three-week tour of the Soviet Union in the Summer of 1947. The writer of the review appeared to doubt Steinbeck's ability to portray life in Soviet Russia authoritatively since he was there for such a short period of time. (100-10622406)

In the reports of the Special Committee on Un-American Activities, 78th Congress, Second Session, House Report No. 1311 on page 101, it is pointed out that "The National Maritime Union of America has toed the Communist Party line through all its changes in recent years. The ships of the American Merchant marines are being supplied with libraries for the seamen to read while at sea, and the National Maritime Union's educational department is responsible for the selection of the books. John Steinbeck's 'Grapes of Wrath' is naturally present, as it would be in any communist's selection." (57-407-424)

The "Daily Worker" issue of April 1, 1955, and the "People's World" issue of April 7, 1955, carried articles relating to a review by John Steinbeck of Matusow's "False Witness" which originally appeared in the April 2nd issue of the "Saturday Review of Literature." In the article captioned "Death of a Racket," Steinbeck speaks with "harsh contempt" of the "anticommunist hired informer." (100-375988-A; "Daily Worker" 4/1/55)

The foregoing information is furnished to you as a result of your request for an FBI file check and is not to be construed as a clearance or a nonclearance of the individual involved. This information is furnished for your use and should not be disseminated outside of your agency.

Note: This memo marked Secret inasmuch as material in paragraph two from State Department was so marked on their communication; information re Steinbeck's furnished USIA on 4/1/54.

Orig. And one to CG

By April, 1957, the Steinbeck file has grown to 12 italic-type single-spaced pages. There appears to be 60 paragraphs in this report (part of the beginning paragraph and six full paragraphs have been redacted).

Of these 60 paragraphs, at least nine paragraphs begin:

> *A confidential informant who has furnished reliable information in the past . . .*

Six paragraphs being with the title or a key reference to *The Daily Worker,* the U.S. Communist newspaper.

At least five paragraphs begin with a reference to the U.S. House of Representatives Committee on Un-American Activities (75th Congress, 1939), or a similar State of California legislative committee.

How detailed (or trivial) was the surveillance of John Steinbeck? The bottom of page five contains this paragraph:

> *The United States Office of Censorship advised by letter dated July 4, 1944 that John Steinbeck, 18 East 14th Street, New York City, had received the February 12, year not given, issue of the "Moscow News," a newspaper published in Russia.*

The entire April, 1957 report on John Steinbeck appears here; original pages also appear in the Appendix of this book.

April 12, 1957
John Ernst Steinbeck

[REDACTED] Steinbeck has never been investigated by this Bureau, however, the files of this Bureau contain the following information:

Steinbeck was born at Salinas, California, February 27, 1902. He graduated from Salinas High School in 1918 and was a student at Stanford University for five years but did not graduate. He married Carol Henning in 1930 and was divorced from her in March, 1943. He married Gwyn Conger on March 29, 1943, and Elaine Scott on December 28, 1950. He has been the author of a number of books and was awarded Pulitzer prize in 1940. Among the books for which he is most noted are "Tortilla Flat," 1935; "Of Mice and Men," 1937; "Grapes of Wrath," 1939; "The Moon Is Down," 1942; "Cannery Row," 1945; "The Wayward Bus," 1947; and "A Russian Journal," 1948. He was also employed as a war correspondent and as a writer for the "New York Herald-Tribune" during 1943, 1944, 1947 and 1948. (100-106224-7)

A Special Committee on Un-American Activities of the United States House of Representatives, 75th Congress, published a report in 1939 captioned "Investigation of Un-American Propaganda Activities in the United States." On Page 1996 under the heading of Western Writers Congress, information was set out that during the Fall of 1936 a group of liberal and communistic writers issued a call for a conference to be held in San Francisco, California, on November 13, 1936, which conference continued throughout the following day. This report indicated that one of the sponsors of this

Congress was John Steinbeck.

A confidential informant who has furnished reliable information in the past advised in 1940 that John Steinbeck was one of the writers who attended the Western Writers Congress in 1936.

The Western Writers Congress was described as a communist front by the Special Committee on Un-American Activities in its report dated March 19, 1944.

A confidential informant who has furnished reliable information in the past advised in 1944 that Sam Darcy was in Russia in 1937 and that Darcy had corresponded with Ella Winter. The informant stated that a letter from Darcy in March, 1937, indicated he was pleased to hear about "Steinbeck's new book." The informant stated Darcy commented that Steinbeck could write and with the education "I am told you and our friends have been giving him, he ought to make the grade better than he did in his early book." The informant furnished no additional information to identify the Steinbeck mentioned and it is not known if this person is identical with the subject of your inquiry. (highly confidential source; 100-18610-56 – pg 29)

The "Times-Herald," a daily newspaper published in Washington, D.C., on May 9, 1953, contained an article reflecting that Herbert A. Philbrick before a United States Senate Investigation Committee had named Ella Winter, the Australian born wife of Donald Ogden Stewart, as one of twenty-three men and women communists in Massachusetts. Additional information concerning Ella Winter Stewart was forwarded to you on June 4, 1952, in the report of Special Agent [REDACTED] which was dated February 18, 1952. (100-18610-A & 222)

A confidential informant who has furnished reliable information in the past advised in 1941 that Samuel Adams Darcy had stated in 1941 that he had traveled abroad in 1935 as he had been elected by the Communist Party in the United States as a representative to the Congress of the Communist International held in Moscow, Russia. Informant advised that Darcy had also returned to the United States in approximately May, 1937. [REDACTED] San Francisco, California; 61-6593-209)

The Committee on Un-American Activities of the United States House of Representatives, 83rd Congress, in a report captioned "Investigation of Communist Activities in the Los Angeles Area , Part 6" contains a statement of Roland William Kibbee, which he furnished to a staff member of the Committee on June 2, 1953. On Page 2329 and 2330 of the above-described report appears information which Kibbee furnished in answer to the question, "What caused your disillusionment wit the Communist Party?" Kibbee stated "I can remember in my own case it even was involved more or less with the theory of the Communist Party and not outside working in organizations . . . Several of the contradictions that arose troubled me a great deal . . .

"I remember John Steinbeck who wrote, I thought, a most effective novel about the agricultural workers in the San Joaquim Valley, or, take it a step further, that the man did more for them than anyone else. A motion picture was made of the very sorry situation that existed there. I recall that John Steinbeck was at odds with the Communist Party. I can't say just how. It was a question of hearing them attacked into work deplored and too bad he doesn't see the light, and so forth, and these things troubled me a great deal . . ." In this statement Kibbee admitted membership in the Communist Party for approximately two years beginning in approximately 1937. (61-7582-1975)

A pamphlet entitled "Their Blood Is Strong" by John Steinbeck was published in April, 1938, by the Simon J. Lubin Society of California, Incorporated. The Simon J. Lubin Society was "deeply appreciative of the cooperation received from the San Francisco News, who in October of 1936 published the seven chapters that form the bulk of this pamphlet; and especially grateful to John Steinbeck for his permission to use this material." (61-7559-2-999)

The California Committee on Un-American Activities in its report published in 1943 described the Simon J. Lubin Society, Incorporated, as a communist front for California Agrcrian penetration, which was organized in the Fall of 1936 by Unit 104 of the Professional Section of the Communist Party. (California Committee 1943 report — pg 86)

On Page 148 of the same California Committee report appears information furnished by Rena M. Vale. Vale advised that the Southwest Unit of the Federal Theaters, which was composed of communists, had corresponded with the Simon J.

Lubin Society in San Francisco, California, to obtain research material which that organization had turned over to John Steinbeck for his book (then unnamed) "Grapes of Wrath" and which Steinbeck had returned. She advised that when the material arrived she had examined it carefully and found notes in handwriting signed by John Steinbeck, which appeared to be field notes on migratory workers. (California Committee Report, 1943, pg. 148)

A pamphlet captioned "Writers Take Sides" was published by the League of American Writers, 381 4th Avenue, New York, New York, in May, 1938, and was described as being letters about the war in Spain from 418 American authors. On Page 56 of this pamphlet appeared a letter from John Steinbeck, the author of "Of Mice and Men" and "Tortilla Flat." (61-7561-2-87)

The "Daily Worker," an east coast communist newspaper, on April 25, 1939, contained an article captioned "Noted Writers Back Fight for Art Projects." The article reflected that 38 prominent writers, including John Steinbeck, had made public a letter urging support of the Federal Arts Project and indicated that the individuals were acting on their behalf as well as on behalf of the League of American Writers. (61-7551-183 X 10)

The "Daily Worker" of September 7, 1939, contained an article captioned "U.S. Writers League Ends Summer Session in South." The article reflected that a two-week session for student writers, which was held under the auspices of the League of American Writers had just concluded. The article described the League of American

Writers as a cultural nonpartisan organization and indicated that one of the vice presidents of the organization was John Steinbeck.

The League of American Writers has been designated by the Attorney General of the United States pursuant to Executive Order 10450. (61-7559-667812)

The records of the Department of State, State of New York, in 1941 reflected a certificate of incorporation was filed in 1939 for the League of American Writers, Incorporated. John Steinbeck, Route 1, Box 95D, Los Angeles, California, was one of the directors who was appointed to act until the first annual meeting of the corporation. (100-7322-8)

The "Los Angeles Times," a daily newspaper published in Los Angeles, California, on January 23, 1941, contained an article which reflected that John Steinbeck of Los Gratos, [sic] California, was one of the California directors of the League of American Writers, which organization was dedicated to the advancement of peace and democracy as against fascism and reaction. (100-7322-16)

The report of the hearings before a Subcommittee of the Committee on Foreign Relations of the United States Senate, 81st Congress, on Page 1504 contained information attributed to "The New York Times" of January 31, 1939. The material was an open letter to the Government and people of the United States which urged that the embargo against the Spanish Republic be lifted. John Steinbeck appeared as one of the persons urging that the Spanish embargo be lifted. The article ended with a coupon which urged that all individuals fill out the coupon and forward it to the Washington Committee to Lift Spanish Embargo, Room 100, 1410 M Street, Northwest, Washington, D.C. (121-23278-267X12)

The Washington Committee to Lift Spanish Embargo was cited as a communist front in the 1948 report of the California committee on Un-American Activities.

In 1950 a confidential informant who has furnished reliable information in the past and who was an admitted member of the Communist Party until 1945 advised that Carey McWilliams was the author of the book "Factories in the Field" published in 1939, which book was the foundation of John Steinbeck's book captioned "Grapes of Wrath." The informant advised that when this book was published he had received information from the Communist Party leaders that McWilliams was under communist discipline. The informant stated that this information had a great deal to do with the way the book was handled as well as Steinbeck's book, because McWilliams at that time was supposedly making a communist of Steinbeck. (Louis Budenz, concealed 400; 100-998-77)

A confidential informant who has furnished reliable information in the past advised in 1940 that the Committee to Aid Agricultural Workers was organized under the leadership of John Steinbeck, the author of "Grapes of Wrath," and that Steinbeck was chairman of the Committee. The informant stated that the Committee had the support of many prominent people in California and that in the informant's opinion, they were all people who had been active in behalf of communist united front organizations. ([REDACTED] 100-3-23-16)

A confidential informant who has furnished reliable information in the past advised in 1941 that the name of John Steinbeck, Route 1, Box 95D, Los Gratos, [sic] California, appeared in the active indices of the National Federation for Constitutional Liberties. ([REDACTED] 100-1170-49)

A representative of another Government agency advised in 1944 that various pieces of literature published in Russia, including daily newspapers from Moscow, Russia, had arrived in the United States during 1942 and part of 1943. The informant advised that some of this material was addressed to John Steinbeck in care of Elizabeth R. Otis, 18 East 41st Street, New York, New York. ([REDACTED] of ONI; 65-1674-809)

The United States Office of Censorship advised by letter dated July 4, 1944, that John Steinbeck, 18 East 41st Street, New York City, had received the February 12, year not given, issue of the "Moscow news," a newspaper published in Russia. (65-49005-81

The report of the Special Committee on Un-American Activities of the United States House of Representatives, published on March 29, 1944, and captioned "Investigation of Un-American Propaganda Activities in the United States" on Page 101 contained the following: "The National Maritime Union of America, . . . has toed the Communist Party line through all its changes in recent years. (57-407-424)

"These ships of the American Merchant Marine are being supplied with libraries for the seamen to read while at sea . . . John Steinbeck's "Grapes of Wrath" is naturally present, as it would be in any Communists' selection. . ."

[FOUR PARAGRAPHS REDACTED]

A confidential informant who has furnished reliable information in the past advised in May, 1945, that the American Youth for Democracy in a list captioned "Recommended Reading List for A.I.D." contained the book entitled "The Moon is Down" by John Steinbeck. 785 Broad Street, Newark, N.J.; 61-777-3-60)

The American Youth for Democracy has been designated by the Attorney General of the United States pursuant to Executive Order 10450.

A confidential informant who has furnished reliable information in the past advised in 1945 that letters had been prepared to be sent to John Steinbeck, among others, requesting that he prepare a testimonial to the valiant Spanish exiles and the work of the Joint Anti-Fascist Refugee Committee. The letter requested a 75-word statement be prepared to be made a part of a leaflet and with an attached photograph it was hoped that such statements would enlist the widest possible mass support for the campaign. (Highly confidential source; 100-7061-923)

The Joint Anti-Fascist Refugee Committee has been designated by the Attorney General of the United States pursuant to Executive Order 10450.

A confidential informant who has furnished reliable information in the past advised in April,

1946, that the National Council of American-Soviet Friendship was planning to give a reception on May 5, 1946, in New York City in honor of three visiting Soviet literary figures. The informant advised that one of the persons indicated to receive an invitation to the reception was John Steinbeck, the novelist. ([REDACTED] 100-14694-795)

The National Council of American-Soviet Friendship has been designated by the Attorney General of the United States pursuant to Executive Order 10450.

"The New York Times" on February 21, 1946, contained an article reflecting the formation of a cooperative publishing concern under the name of the Associated Magazine Contributors, Incorporated. The article set forth the initial list of owner-contributors, which included the name of John Steinbeck. (123-11674-13)

The 1948 report of the California Committee on Un-American Activities reflected that in addition to completely communist-controlled and dominated publications there was also a long list of Trade Union, racial, minority, liberal and special interests publications into which communists had infiltrated. The report reflected that the communist influence was established through such news services as the Associated Magazine Contributors, Incorporated, and others. (100-15252-39 - pg 39)

[ONE PARAGRAPH REDACTED]

The October 24, 1947, "Daily Worker," an east coast communist newspaper, published an article captioned "Found Soviets Eager for Peace, Capa,

Steinbeck Tell Trib Forum." This article indicated that Capa read a joint report by himself and John Steinbeck at the Herald Tribune Forum. This report purportedly stated that the Russian people were destroyed and hurt much more than any others that they, Capa and Steinbeck, had seen during their many years on the battle fields. The report further indicated that the Russian masses would strongly approve the halt of the "vicious and insane games" of recrimination between Russia and the U.S. It was indicated that the Russians were particularly interested in hearing about "the persecution of liberals" in America. (100-106224)

The "Daily Worker" on April 16, 1948, contained a book review of John Steinbeck's "A Russian Journal," which was described as being a book containing photographs by Robert Capa, which had been published by the Viking Press in New York, New York. The article reflected "John Steinbeck's warm sympathy for people, as evidenced in his 'A Russian Journal,' (published today) is the one positive feature of an account of a visit to the Soviet Union which is otherwise overrun with frivolous provincialism and a coy disinclination to face political realities . . .

"What is one to say of a writer to whom the distinctive characteristic of American capitalist society is that it provides a government of 'checks and balances'? Or of the naivete which has it that 'our government is designed to keep anyone from getting too much power or, having got it, from keeping it'? And, 'we agreed,' Steinbeck writes solemnly, 'that this makes our country function more slowly, but that it certainly makes it function more surely . . .'

"One could go on quoting Steinbeck, but what for? A Russian Journal is much more enlightening about the kind of culture which develops such intellectual Sad Sackery than about the Soviet Union . . ."

The "New Leader," a weekly magazine, on August 21, 1948, contained an article captioned "Steinbeck Sans Wrath," which was a book review of "A Russian Journal," which was written by Steinbeck and contained pictures by Robert Capa. The article reflected that "Mr. Steinbeck has joined the fraternity of vodka visitors. For three weeks he toured the Soviet Union under the subtle guidance of VOKS, the government agency for 'cultural liaison,' . . ."The article reflected he had attended the "celebration of the 800th anniversary of Moscow with Louis Aragon, the French Stalinist writer" and had visited the country home of "such Soviet millionaires as Alexander Korneichuk — and concludes that the Russians have plenty to eat; he even states that the quality of Russian clothing improved during the few weeks he spent in Russia . . ."

The article further reflected "most startling, perhaps, is Steinbeck's own attitude toward the Soviet Union. His book is full of what Koestler would call false equations. When Capa is stopped from taking pictures at a lend-leased tractor plant in Stalingrad, Steinbeck reminds us that foreigners may not photograph Oak Ridge either. In his mind 'Moscowitis' and 'Washingtonitis' cancel each other out. When he admits that the collective farm he was shown put on a big show for him, he insists that 'any Kansas farmer' would do the same for his guests . . .

"Steinbeck used to be known as a man with a strong social conscience. The 'Grapes of Wrath' and 'Tortilla Flat' were full of righteous moral indignation about social and economic injustice. In 'The Moon is Down' Steinbeck made a heated if somewhat pedestrian attack on totalitarian aggression and conquest. Those were the days when Steinbeck could be counted upon to stand up and wield his pen in behalf of democracy and freedom. Even today had he gone to Spain or China, he would surely not have come back to write a book in order to demonstrate that the 'Chinese people want good lives and comfort' or that 'the Spaniards like peace.'"

A confidential informant who has furnished reliable information in the past advised in 1948 that the firm of World Video, Incorporated, was chartered in New York State on December 18, 1947, and that the firm prepared television programs. The officers of the firm include John Steinbeck as vice president and Robert Capa as assistant vice president. ([REDACTED] NYC; 100-340922-111)

[ONE PARAGRAPH REDACTED]

The "New York Herald-Tribune of May 18, 1948, contained an article captioned "Women's Rally in Rome Hears Russia Praised." The article, which was datelined Rome, May 17, reflected that the meeting was that of the Democratic Women's International Federation, whose aim was to fight "American, British and French imperialists and warmongers." He article reflected that the chief American delegate, Mrs. Muriel Draper, chairman of the women's section of the American National Committee for American-Soviet Friendship mentioned several persons converted to "the camp of war and anti-Sovietism," which included John Steinbeck.

The "Los Angeles Examiner," a daily newspaper published in Los Angeles, California, on June 11, 1948, contained an article reflecting that Ring Lardner, Jr., had signed a contract with John Steinbeck and others to write a film version of Steinbeck's story "Pastures of Heaven." The article reflected this was the first Hollywood employment given "any of the 'un-friendly ten' since their refusal to answer the Communist question in Washington last fall." (100-295885-11)

The "Daily Worker" on April 1, 1955, contained an article captioned "John Steinbeck Takes a Look at Matusow and 'Death of a Racket.'" The article was a review of an article by Steinbeck which appeared in the April 2, 1955, issue of "Saturday Review." The article reflected that Steinbeck's article captioned "Death of a Racket" was based on the book "False Witness" written by Harvey Matusow. Steinbeck's article reportedly stated:

"The Matusow testimony to anyone who will listen places a bouquet of forget-me-nots on the grave of McCarthy. The ridiculousness of the whole series of investigations now becomes apparent, even to what a friend of mine used to call peanut-munchers. Matusow will have a much greater effect than he knows. What follows cannot be worse and may be better. It will surely be funny."

The "Daily Worker" article continues, "It is impossible not to be moved by this kind of statement of an angered scorn which, if the record is to be kept straight, itself participated in, and helped to create, that very climate, those same 'winds of the time' as Steinbeck puts it, 'when certain basic nonsense was allowed to pass unnoticed.' For Steinbeck was taken in tow by the Cold War leadership to such an extent that he did not scruple even to lend the authority of his literary achievement to State Department broadcasts in fascist Spain, Italy, Vienna, etc."

The article continued "Steinbeck's contempt for the 'certain basic nonsense' which was believed under the influence of the Cold War hysteria does not lead him to a reflection of the Big Lie about the working-class Communist party. He still says that the Communists approve of 'the climate of disunity and suspicion which has haunted us for the last few years,' and that Communists 'would much rather keep the investigations going with their harvest of fear and disruption.' . . . It suffices that John Steinbeck has expressed sentiments which a literary artist with a sense of responsibility for his nation cannot long silence without crushing his talent. . . " (100-374988-A)

For additional information concerning Steinbeck you may desire to contact the Assistant Chief of Staff, Intelligence, of the United States Army and the Department of State.

The above information is furnished to you as

a result of your request for a name check and should not be construed as a clearance or non-clearance of captioned individual. The information is furnished for your use and should not be disseminated outside of your agency.

Note: Steinbeck never investigated by Bureau. Steinbeck sent letter to Attorney General Biddle in 1942 which contained "Do you suppose you could ask Edgar's boys to stop stepping on my heels? They think I'm an enemy alien. It's getting tiresome." The AG was advised on 5/21/42 that Steinbeck was not being and had never been investigated.

The Attorney General's office telephonically requested the Bureau's file on Steinbeck on 10/27/42 and was advised only information available was two pamphlets. G-2 investigated Steinbeck in 1943 and it was recommended Steinbeck not be given Army Commission. (100-106224)

John Steinbeck's *The Grapes of Wrath* is full of dozens and dozens of references to the Bible:

• the journey of the Joad family to their promised land of California echoes the journey of the tribe of Israel from Egypt, their land of bondage, toward freedom;

• when Jim Casey (with the initials J.C.), the preacher, is killed toward the end of the book he says "they don't know what they're doin'. . ." a paraphrase of the words of Christ;

• when Rose of Sharon's baby is born dead

she was unable (as was typical of the plight of Okies throughout the west) to bury it in a local cemetery; she put it on a home-made raft and pushed it downstream, toward the nearest city with the admonition "go show them what happened to you . . .", which is a black reversal of the Biblical story of the baby Moses found in the bullrushes.

And there are many, many other such references, clearly stated or implied, throughout *The Grapes of Wrath.*

In the late 1950s, Steinbeck complied a list of individuals from the Bible who could not be then admitted into the United States, because of their background. (For those who knew him, or who have read him carefully, this was Steinbeck being Steinbeck.)

Columnist George E. Sokolsky, writing in the (now-defunct) *The New York Journal-American* newspaper, comments about Steinbeck's list. Although Steinbeck's original essay did not appear in the FBI files under his name, Sokolsky's column did, date stamped JUN 10 1957 and JUN 12 1957. And the FBI files contains the same column, from *The Washington Post,* date stamped JUN 10 1957, JUN 12 1957 and JUN 13 1957. The first column appears here:

These Days:
Steinbeck's List Proves Nothing

BY GEORGE E. SOKOLSKY

John Steinbeck, who writes novels and things, has compiled a list of those who could not enter the United States under its present laws. He says that it is not a joke and, of course, as it is published in the erudite "Saturday Review," it cannot possibly be a joke, but it does seem to be a futile occupation for so noble a mind. After all, every country determines who is to be admitted to it, just as every well-ordered household decides what kind of persons it wants to invite to dinner.

I shall take the first five names on Steinbeck's list as an example of his thinking and because the entire list would add nothing to the reader's knowledge, except perhaps to wonder at Steinbeck's logic:

"NAME CHARGE
ADAM Morals
CAIN Murder
NOAH Alcoholism, cruelty to animals
SAUL Assault with intent to kill
DAVID Revolution"

Of course, John Steinbeck has a perfect right to understand the book of Genesis, in the bible, as he chooses, in whatever language he has learned to read it. However, if he accepts the theories of the Hebrews on the subject of Adam, that progenitor of the human race bears no moral stigma, except the Fall which made us humans instead of angels, seraphim and other disembodied spirits. So, Steinbeck's trouble is not that he does not understand a Semitic folk-tale, but its mystical meaning is beyond him altogether.

As for Cain, naturally we should keep him out. A man who kills his brother is undesirable in any society.

Would Steinbeck have him admitted? Would he build an arch of triumph for him? I saw a preview of Leo McCarey's picture, "An Affair to Remember," and I could not help thinking that these are perfectly normal, healthy human beings—nothing dirty about a one of them. Does John Steinbeck object to such a picture? Must we welcome murderers to our company to please Steinbeck?

Teaches Respect for Parents

His next objectionable character is Noah, who built the Ark. The story of Noah is particularly significant in Hebrew folklore because it teaches respect for parents. Noah liked his wine and he lay asleep, uncovered and improperly exposed. Shem covered the shame of his father with respectful delicacy. Perhaps Steinbeck does not, in this age of sophisticated ignorance, grasp the beauty of this tale, or even know of it.

So we come to Saul, having skipped over many Biblical characters that Steinbeck might have used if he knew of them, for instance, Lot and his wife, and all the progenitors of the Semitic peoples who were polygamists and each had several wives which was not prohibited by local law or custom. Saul was a king at a time when kings ruled autocratically and when a king had power of life and death over his subjects. The Hebrews, however, had a control over the kings, namely that there were prophets, Holy men who were regarded by the people as being the voice of God. Saul was bawled out by a prophet when his conduct became too oppressive. After all, if we admitted King Saud, a descendant of Ishmael, probably way back an Edomite, and housed him in Blair House as a guest of the nation, we would surely have admitted Saul. The precedents are against Steinbeck. Also we admitted

Haile Selassie of Ethiopia, a descendant of David by way of Solomon and the Queen of Sheba.

No, he objects to David as a revolutionist, which David was not at all because he was obeying the will of God, which cannot be said of Lenin or Trotsky who denied God. David killed Goliath and saved is people which was a very proper thing to do then as now. Thereupon David and the King's son, Jonathan, became pals. But it was the Lord's intent that David should rule and it is so clearly stated. And one reason was that David was a very holy man who wrote many psalms, some of which have come down to us to this day and which are read at all Jewish and Christian religious services.

It is perfectly clear that of John Steinbeck's first five, four could have come into the United States and would have been received either by President Eisenhower or John foster Dulles. The fifth, who killed his brother, Steinbeck can keep for himself.

In late November, 1958 the FBI received another request for information about Steinbeck. This one-page response (and a copy) was sent December 1, 1958, presumably to the United States Information Agency, as the response carries the annotation on the bottom left corner "Orig and one to USIA."

December 1, 1958

John E. Steinbeck
Born: February 27, 1902
Salinas, California

TOP SECRET

You are referred to our memorandum dated March 1, 1954, concerning the captioned individual.

The April 1, 1955, issue of the "Daily Worker" and the April 7, 1955 issue of the "People's World" carried articles relating to a review by John Steinbeck of Matusow's "False Witness" which originally appeared in the April 2 issue of the "Saturday Review of Literature." In the article captioned "Death of a Racket," Steinbeck speaks with "harsh contempt" of the "Anti-Communist Hired Informer." (100-375988-A Daily Worker 4/1/55)

The "Daily Worker" was an east coast communist newspaper which suspended publication on January 13, 1958. The "daily People's World" has been cited by the Special Committee on Un-American Activities, House Report 1311, dated March 29, 1944 as "the official organ of the Communist Party on the west coast."

The foregoing information is furnished to you as a result of your request for an FBI file check and is not to be construed as a clearance or a nonclearance of the individual involved. This information is loaned for your use and is not to be disseminated outside of your agency.

Orig and one to USIA

After the publication of Steinbeck's *The Winter of Our Discontent* in 1961, the FBI critiqued the book in terms of the FBI image in the novel.

September 13, 1961

Mr. DeLoach:

Re: Mention of FBI in the Book "The Winter of our Discontent" by John Steinbeck

The above book, a recent Literary Guild selection, is a novel laid in the fictitious town of New Baytown, New York, and concerns the problems of a young grocery store clerk whose family had at one time been among the leaders of the community. The book is written in the first-person as though being told by the "hero." At the beginning of the book he describes various persons of the town including one Stonewall Jackson Smith, the Chief of Police, whom he characterizes as being of above average intelligence for the town and who "even took the FBI training at Washington, D.C."

Later in the story, just a weekend before the local elections, the Grand Jury indicts the city manager and other high officials for corruption, etc. Immediately prior to the announcement of the indictments, Chief "Stoney" Smith had made a trip to the State Capitol and in a subsequent conversation between the Chief and the grocer clerk, in which the Chief is clearly suffering from a guilty conscience, it becomes evident that he has been excluded from the indictments because he chose to "turn state's evidence," so to speak, and furnish information against the other town officials.

TOP SECRET

OBSERVATION

While Steinbeck does not belabor the fact that the Chief of Police is FBI trained, nevertheless a careful reader cannot fail to recall the reference in the initial introduction to the Chief when his behavior concerning the indictments comes up.

By contrast, Steinbeck's references to a Justice Department investigator who appears in the story investigating the illegal entry into the United States of one of the townspeople are of the highest caliber.

RECOMMENDATION

For information.

One additional page was deleted entirely prior to the release of the Steinbeck file as a Freedom of Information document. This page appears in the Appendix.

In 1964, the Central Intelligence Agency requests a file on Steinbeck. The FBI furnishes the following. On the bottom left corner is the annotation: "Original and 1-CIA."

March 4, 1964

John Ernst Steinbeck
Born: February 27, 1902
Salinas, California

A review of FBI files reveals the following information which may pertain to captioned individual.

Enclosed is a copy of an article appearing on page five of the "Worker" midweek edition dated October 29, 1963, captioned "Steinbeck in Moscow Impressed by Progress."

The "Worker" is an East Coast communist publication.

Your attention is directed to the following reports and memoranda which have been sent to your agency:

Memorandum dated April 12, 1957, captioned "John Ernst Steinbeck" sent April 15, 1957.

Report dated August 24, 1959, by SAA [REDACTED] at New York captioned "Bulgarian Funds, New York Division" sent August 31, 1959.

Memorandum dated May 26, 1960, Chicago, Illinois, captioned [REDACTED], Internal Security-PO sent June 8, 1960.

Report dated February 15, 1964, at New York, by SA [REDACTED] captioned "Russky Golos Publishing Company."

(100-106224-10, 65-34794-239, 105-81470-7, 100-39588-276)

Enclosure

Original & 1-CIA
Request Received-2-27-64

A six-page single-spaced italic summary of Steinbeck's career appears in the FBI files dated May 28, 1964. Sections of page three — about one-third of a page — one paragraph on page four and one paragraph or end section on page six were redacted prior to release. The summary appears here and the original pages appear in the Appendix. This six-page summary/profile rehashes all the old *Daily Worker* citations from previous documents.

This document contains the same key sentence seen in previous FBI documents:

> John Ernst Steinbeck has never been the subject of investigation by the FBI.

But in fact, the documents in the FBI files have been substantial and the FBI had been, at the very least, the central clearinghouse and repository for Steinbeck files, circulated to the U.S.I.A., the C.I.A. and other governmental agencies.

And, by 1964, it had been 22 years since John Steinbeck wrote to Attorney General Biddle:

> Do you suppose you could ask Edgar's boys to stop stepping on my heels? They think I am an enemy alien. It is getting tiresome.

The second-to-the-end paragraph on page six reads:

> In 1959, a reliable source advised the FBI that during July of that year John Steinbeck, in care of McIntosh and Otis, Inc. New York, New York, had been paid the sum of $188.70 from the New York account of the National Bank of Bulgaria. It was not known to the source if this individual was identical with John Ernst Steinbeck.

Two thoughts here: 1) Any quick check by any FBI agent would have confirmed that the firm of McIntosh and Otis had been John Ernst Steinbeck's literary agents for virtually all of his active career; and 2) Since a payment was made directly to McIntosh and Otis, the check was probably for book royalties to Steinbeck from Bulgaria.

May 20, 1964

John Ernst Steinbeck

John Ernst Steinbeck has never been the subject of investigation by the FBI.

Mr. Steinbeck was born at Salinas, California, on February 27, 1902. He was a student at Stanford University for five years but did not graduate. He married Carol Henning in 1930 and was divorced from her in March, 1943. He married Gwyn Conger on March 29, 1943, and Elaine Scott on December 28, 1950. He has been the author of a number of books and was awarded the Pulitzer prize in 1940. He was also employed as a war correspondent and as a writer for the "New York Herald Tribune" during 1943, 1944, 1947 and 1948.

According to the annual report of the House of representatives Committee on Un-American Activities published in 1939, during the Fall of 1936 a group of liberal and communist writers issued a call for a conference to be held in San Francisco, California, on November 13, 1936, under the auspices of the Western Writers' Congress. The report indicated that one of the sponsors of this Congress was John Steinbeck. A reliable informant of the FBI advised in 1948 that John Steinbeck was one of the writers who attended the Western Writers' Congress in 1936. In 1944, this Congress was described by the House Committee on Un-American Activities (HCUA) as a communist front.

According to a reliable informant of the FBI, San Darcy, in 1937, indicated to Ella Winter that he was pleased to hear about "Steinbeck's new book." Darcy commented that Steinbeck could write and with the education "I am told you and our friends have been giving him, he ought to make the grade better than he did in his early book." The informant furnished no additional information to identify the Steinbeck mentioned, and it is not known if this person is identical to John Ernst Steinbeck.

[One paragraph REDACTED]

A pamphlet entitled "Their Blood Is Strong" by John Steinbeck was published in April, 1933, by the Simon J. Lubin Society of California, Incorporated (SJLSCI). This pamphlet consisted of material which Steinbeck had published elsewhere and which had been reprinted in pamphlet form with Steinbeck's permission. The California Committee on Un-American Activities (CCUA) in its report published in 1948 described the SJLSCI as a communist front for California agrarian penetration.

A pamphlet captioned "Writers Take Sides" was published by the League of American Writers

(LAW), New York, New York, in May, 1938, and was described as containing letters about the war in Spain from 418 American authors. On Page 56 of this pamphlet there appeared a letter from John Steinbeck. The "Daily Worker," an East coast communist newspaper, on April 23, 1939, contained an article noting that 38 prominent writers, including John Steinbeck, had made public a letter urging support of the Federal Arts Project and indicating that the individuals were acting on their behalf as well as on the behalf of the LAW. The article noted in one of the vice presidents of the organization was John Steinbeck.

The records of the Department of State, State of New York, in 1941 reflected a certificate of incorporation was filed in 1939 for the LAW. John Steinbeck, of Los Angeles, California, was one of the directors who was appointed to act until the first annual meeting of the corporation.

The LAW has been cited as subversive pursuant to Executive Order 10450.

The report of the hearings before a subcommittee of the Committee on Foreign Relations of the United States Senate, 81st Congress, on Page 1504, contained information attributed to "The New York Times" of January 31, 1939, which consisted of an open letter urging that the embargo against Spain be lifted. John Steinbeck appeared as one of the persons urging that the Spanish embargo be lifted, and it was indicated that the organization sponsoring the plea was the Washington Committee to Lift Spanish Embargo. This organization was cited as a communist front in the 1943 report of the CCUA.

In 1950, a reliable informant of the FBI advised that Carey McWilliam was the author of the book, "Factories in the Field," published in 1939, which was the foundation of John Steinbeck's book, "Grapes of Wrath." According to the informant, McWilliams was under communist discipline and this had a great deal to do with the way this book was handled as well as Steinbeck's book because McWilliam at that time was supposedly making a communist out of Steinbeck.

In 1940, a reliable informant of the FBI advised that the Committee To Aid Agricultural Workers was organized under the leadership of John Steinbeck, and it had the support of many prominent people in California. In the informant's opinion, they were all people who had been active in behalf of "communist united front organizations."

In 1941, a reliable source advised the FBI that the name of John Steinbeck, Los Gatos, California, appeared in the active indices of the National Federation for Constitutional Liberties. This organization has been cited as subversive pursuant to Executive Order 10450.

In 1944, the records of the Office of Naval Intelligence indicated that one John Steinbeck, New York, New York, ad received literature and daily newspapers from Moscow, Russia, during 1942 and 1943. The United States Office of Censorship advised in 1944 that this same John Steinbeck had received a copy of the "Moscow News," a newspaper published in Russia.

The report of the House of Representatives Committee on Un-American Activities, published on March 29, 1944, described The National Maritime Union of America a shaving "toed the Communist Party line through all its changes in recent years." The report continued, "These ships of the American Merchant Marine are being supplied with libraries for the seamen to read while at sea . . . John Steinbeck's 'Grapes of Wrath' is naturally present, as it would be in any Communists' selection."

[Two paragraphs REDACTED]

A reliable informant of the FBI advised in May, 1945, that the American Youth for Democracy, an organization which has been cited as subversive within the purview of Executive Order 10450, issued a list of recommended reading which contained the book entitled "The Moon is Down" by John Steinbeck.

In 1945, a reliable informant of the FBI advised that letters had been prepared to be sent to John Steinbeck, among others, requesting that he prepare a testimonial to the "valiant Spanish exiles and the work of the Joint Anti-Fascist Refugee Committee." This organization has been cited as subversive within the purview of Executive Order 10450.

A reliable source, in April, 1946, advised the FBI that the National Council of American-Soviet Friendship in New York City was planning to give a reception in New York City in honor of three visiting Soviet literary figures. According to the informant, John Steinbeck was indicated to be one of those persons who would receive an invitation to attend this reception.

"The New York Times," on February 21, 1946,

described the formation of a cooperative publishing concern under the name of the Associated Magazine Contributors, Incorporated. The article set forth the initial list of owner-contributors, which included the name of John Steinbeck. The 1948 report of the CCUA discussed communist infiltration of various publications. The report reflected that communist influence was established through such news services as the Associated Magazine Contributors, Incorporated, and others.

[One paragraph REDACTED]

The October 24, 1947, issue of the "Daily Worker" contained an article concerning a report which had been read at the Herald Tribune Forum. John Steinbeck was coauthor of this report. The report expressed sympathy for the sufferings of the Russian people during the war and indicated that the Russian masses would strongly approve the halt of the "vicious and insane games" of recrimination between Russia and the United States.

The "Daily Worker" on April 16, 1948, contained a book review of John Steinbeck's "A Russian Journal." The article stated, "John Steinbeck's warm sympathy for people, as evidenced in his 'A Russian Journal,' (published today) is the one positive feature of an account of a visit to the Soviet Union which is otherwise overrun with frivolous provincialism and a coy disinclination to face political realities."

This article continued to criticize Steinbeck for his favorable references to the American form of government, including his statements that "our government is designed to keep anyone from getting too much power or, having got it, from keeping it," and "we agreed that this makes our country function more slowly, but that it certainly makes it function more surely."

The "New Leader," a weekly magazine, on August 21, 1943, also reviewed Steinbeck's "A Russian Journal" and criticized Steinbeck as a Soviet apologist. The article indicated that Steinbeck had visited the homes of millionaires and implied that from this Steinbeck had concluded that the Russians have plenty to eat and that the quality of Russian clothing had improved. The article noted that Steinbeck constantly made excuses for the Russians, and it pointed out that when he admitted that a collective farm had put on a big show for him, he also insisted that "any Kansas farmer" would go the same for his guests.

The "New York Herald Tribune" of May 18, 1945, contained an article concerning a meeting in Rome, Italy, of the Democrat Women's International Federation whose aim was to fight "American, British and French imperialists and warmongers." At this meeting, John Steinbeck was publicly criticized as one of several persons who had been converted to "the camp of war and anti-Sovietism."

The "Los Angeles Examiner," on June 11, 1948, contained an article reflecting that Ring Lardner, Jr., had signed a contract with John Steinbeck and others to write a film version of Steinbeck's story, "Pastures of Heaven." The article reflected that this was the first Hollywood employment given "any of the 'un-friendly ten' since their refusal to answer the communist question in Washington last fall."

The "Daily Worker," on April 1, 1955, contained an article, "John Steinbeck Takes a Look at Matusow and 'Death of a Racket.'" The article was a review of an article Steinbeck had prepared concerning the book, "False Witness," written by Harvey Matusow. The Steinbeck article was obviously critical of Matusow and stated that as a result of Matusow's testimony, the "ridiculousness of the whole series of the investigations now becomes apparent." The "Daily Worker" article was critical of Steinbeck, especially when he asserted that the communists approved of "the climate of disunity and suspicion which has haunted us for the last few years," and that the communists "would much rather keep the investigations going with their harvest of fear and disruption." (100-106224-9)

In 1949, a reliable source advised the FBI that John Steinbeck was on the mailing list of the Japan Council Against Atomic and Hydrogen Bombs. Another reliable source has described this organization as a communist infiltrated organization in Japan. (105-62469-14)

In 1959, a reliable source advised the FBI that during July of that year John Steinbeck, in care of McIntosh and Otis, Inc., New York, New York, had been paid the sum of $188.70 from the New York account of the National Bank of Bulgaria. It was not known to the source of this individual was identical with John Ernst Steinbeck. (65-34794-239)

In April, 1964, a reliable source advised the FBI that on March 12, 1964, John Ernst Steinbeck had received the sum of $420 as an author's fee from the Soviet publication, "Novyi Mir." (65-28939-3046)

[One paragraph REDACTED]

A two-page single-spaced italic summary of Steinbeck's career appears in the FBI files dated July 20, 1965. It is the last entry in the FBI files on John Steinbeck.

Clyde Tolson, who received a copy of this file, was J. Edgar Hoover's second-in-command at the FBI. Cartha "Deke" DeLoach was also a high FBI official. Years later, the FBI must have still been stung by Steinbeck's 1942 letter to Attorney General Biddle, as it is cited in this file.

7-20-65

To: Mr. DeLoach

From: M. A. Jones

Subject: John Ernst Steinbeck

In response to Mr. Tolson's request, the following data is being set out as a result of a check of our files on captioned individual.

Mr. Steinbeck was born at Salinas, California, on February 27, 1902. He was a student at Stanford University for five years but did not graduate. He married Carol Henning in 1930 and was divorced from her in March, 1943. He married Gwyn Conger on March 29, 1943, and Elaine Scott on December 28, 1950. He has been the author of a number of books and was awarded the Pulitzer prize in 1940. He was also employed as a war correspondent and as a writer for the "New York Herald Tribune" during 1943, 1944, 1947 and 1948.

Although he has never been investigated by the FBI, he wrote Attorney General Biddle in May, 1942, as follows: "Do you suppose you could ask Edgar's boys to stop stepping on my heels? They think I am an enemy alien. It is getting tiresome."

Army Intelligence (G-2) investigated Steinbeck during 1943 to determine suitability to hold commission in Army, but was recommended unfavorably. Carol Steinbeck (first wife, divorced 1943), registered as a Communist in California in 1938 to see reaction it would cause. Steinbeck opposed his wife's action, and he was registered as a Democrat.

Steinbeck reportedly associated with communists during early days of his writings, 1936–1941, to gather material for books but was not interested in advancing the cause of the Party. Many of his writings, including "Grapes of Wrath," 1939, were about poverty-stricken migrant workers and portrayed the sordid side of American life. Due to the nature of his writings they were translated into foreign languages and widely distributed by enemies of the United States (both Nazis and Soviets), as examples of life in the United States even though the communists were reportedly at odds with him as they did not feel he adequately portrayed American communists or life in Russia.

He has been connected to a limited extent with various organizations and publications that have been cited by the Department, the House Committee on Un-American Activities or state legislative committees during the period 1936–1946. Some of these organizations included the following: the Western Writers Congress (1936); the League of American Writers (1939); the National Federation for Constitutional Liberties (1941) and the Simon T. Lubin Society, Inc. (1938). In 1938, he organized and served as chairman of the John Steinbeck Committee to Aid Agricultural Workers which was widely supported by communists. Among Communist Party members reportedly attempting to make a communist out of Steinbeck (1937–1940) were Ella Winter, California Communist Party functionary, and Carey McWilliams described by Budenz as under communist discipline. (100-115040)

The "New York Herald Tribune" of May 18, 1948, contained an article concerning a meeting in Rome, Italy, of the Democratic Women's International Federation whose aim was to fight. "American, British and French imperialists and warmongers." At this meeting, John Steinbeck was publicly criticized as one of several persons who had been converted to "the camp of war and anti-Sovietism."

The 4-1-55 issue of the "Daily Worker" contained a review of an article Steinbeck had prepared concerning the book, "False Witness," written by Harvey Matusow in which Steinbeck criticized Matusow's testimony. The "Daily Worker" article was critical of Steinbeck on this occasion because he had asserted that the communists were also responsible for the climate of disunity and suspicion throughout the world during this period.

In 1959, a reliable source advised the FBI that John Steinbeck was on the mailing list of the Japan Council Against Atomic and Hydrogen Bombs. Another reliable source has described this organization as a communist-infiltrated organization in Japan.

In April, 1964, a reliable source advised the FBI that on March 12, 1964, John Ernst Steinbeck had received the sum of $420 as an author's fee from the Soviet publication, "Novyi Mir." (62-5-19610)

RECOMMENDATION:

For information.

Appendix

The following pages are examples of documents in the John Steinbeck FBI files . . .

pp. 114	Short newspaper clipping indicating Steinbeck was the subject of an extortion threat.
115	Memo to the Director, FBI, from the Special Agent in Charge (S.A.C.), San Francisco, indicating that "no investigation is being made" of the extortion attempt and a copy of the SAC's letter to the FBI was forwarded to the Salt Lake City Bureau.
116	Attorney General Biddle memo to J. Edgar Hoover, about "John Steinbeck, the playwright."
117	Steinbeck's letter to Biddle.
118	J. Edgar Hoover's reply to Biddle.
119	The Justice Department asks to see the FBI file on Steinbeck.
120	The FBI's reply to the Justice Department, relayed to J. Edgar Hoover.
121	1942 Citizen complaint about Steinbeck's books. The writer's name is redacted as is an additional name reference.
122-142	G-2's investigation of Steinbeck's character. G-2 ultimate decided that Steinbeck was not a good candidate as an officer in the U.S.

	Armed Services during World War Two.
143	Special Agent in Charge (SAC), of the San Antonio Bureau of the FBI reports Steinbeck entering the country from Mexico, at Brownsville, Texas, April, 1944.
144-145	Another citizen complaint letter about Steinbeck, in the FBI files.
146-147	Newspaper reprint of one chapter from Steinbeck's *A Russian Journal,* in the FBI files.
148	Reply to request for information on Steinbeck from the State Department, 1952.
149-156	File on Steinbeck, with redactions, on latter pages.
157-168	An additional update on Steinbeck, with redactions, in the FBI files.
169	FBI "review" of Steinbeck's *The Winter of Our Discontent,* 1961.
170-171	FBI reply to a request by the White House, for information.
172-177	Last summary file in the Steinbeck archive.

STEINBECK GETS EXTORTION THREAT

SAN JOSE, Cal., May [illegible] — Sheriff's deputies [illegible] today that Novelist John Steinbeck had received a letter and telegram from Reno, Nev. demanding money, [illegible]

Deputies Jack [illegible] and [illegible] said the letter was signed "Maurey B Campbell" and [illegible] The telegram signed "Melancholic Black" [illegible] The deputies [illegible]

[illegible] police and [illegible] are cooperating with the sheriff's office in the investigation.

Letter to Director
From S.A.C. San Francisco

June 13, 1939
- page 2 -

In accordance with Bureau instructions, no investigation is being made at this Division, although copies of this letter and Bureau letter, with enclosure, are being forwarded herewith to the Salt Lake City Field Division for its information only and as a basis for further investigation, should the Bureau desire that office to conduct any investigation at Reno, where the original letter and telegram were apparently written.

Very truly yours,

N.J.L.PIEPER,
Special Agent in Charge

[illegible]
9-173

AIR MAIL
[illegible]

cc: Salt Lake City

TOP SECRET

May 11, 1942

MEMORANDUM FOR MR. HOOVER

Will you note the attached letter of John Steinbeck, the playwright?

Francis Biddle
Attorney General

DEPT. OF JUST.
F. B. I.
FILED-SECURITY UNIT

td

THE BEDFORD
115 East 40th Street
New York

Caledonia 5-1000

Dear Mr. Biddle:

I'm very sorry I haven't been able to see you. Do you suppose you could ask Edgar's boys to stop stepping on my heels? They think I'm an enemy alien. It's getting tiresome.

Congratulations on the S.S. matter,

/s/ John Steinbeck

COPY

100-106224-1

EED:lem
5-18-42

MAY 21 1942

100-106224-1

THE INFORMATION CONTAINED HEREIN IS UNCLASSIFIED

MEMORANDUM FOR THE ATTORNEY GENERAL

Reference is made to your memorandum dated May 11, 1942, transmitting a letter addressed to you by John Steinbeck, in which Steinbeck complained that he was being investigated as an enemy alien by representatives of this Bureau.

I wish to advise that Steinbeck is not being and has never been investigated by this Bureau. His letter to you is returned herewith.

Respectfully,

John Edgar Hoover
Director

Inclosure

SENT FROM D. O.
TIME 2:00
DATE 5-21-42
BY

Mr. Tolson
Mr. E. A. Tamm
Mr. Clegg
Mr. Glavin
Mr. Ladd
Mr. Nichols
Mr. Rosen
Mr. Tracy
Mr. Carson
Mr. Coffey
Mr. Hendon
Mr. Holloman
Mr. McGuire
Mr. Quinn Tamm
Mr. Nease
Miss Gandy

MAY 26 1942

JOHN EDGAR HOOVER
DIRECTOR

Federal Bureau of Investigation
United States Department of Justice
Washington, D. C.

CC-237

Mr. Tolson____
Mr. E. A. Tamm____
Mr. Clegg____
Mr. Glavin____
Mr. Ladd____
Mr. Nichols____
Mr. Rosen____
Mr. Tracy____
Mr. Carson____
Mr. Coffey____
Mr. Hendon____
Mr. Kramer____
Mr. McGuire____
Mr. Harbo____
Mr. Quinn Tamm____
Tele. Room____
Mr. Nease____
Miss Beahm____
Miss Gandy____

EXPEDITE

5:05 P. M.

October 27, 1942

MEMORANDUM FOR MR. E. A. TAMM

ALL INFORMATION CONTAINED
HEREIN IS UNCLASSIFIED
[redacted]

Miss Collins in the Attorney General's office telephoned and advised that the Attorney General wanted to see the Bureau's file on John Steinbeck tomorrow morning (Oct. 28th).

Respectfully,

D. STALCUP.

5:45 P. M. Miss Collins was advised that the Bureau had conducted no investigation concerning John Steinbeck and her attention was called to the Bureau's memorandum of May 21, 1942, in which the Attorney General was so advised.

ds

100-106224-2

12 OCT 28 1942

NOV 7 1942

EX-36

JOHN EDGAR HOOVER
DIRECTOR

Federal Bureau of Investigation
United States Department of Justice
Washington, D. C.
October 30, 1942

OO-287

Mr. Tolson
Mr. E. A. Tamm
Mr. Clegg
Mr. Glavin
Mr. Ladd
Mr. Nichols
Mr. Rosen
Mr. Tracy
Mr. Carson
Mr. Coffey
Mr. Hendon
Mr. Kramer
Mr. McGuire
Mr. Harbo
Mr. Quinn Tamm
Tele. Room
Mr. Nease
Miss Beahm
Miss Gandy

EAT:RBK
Call 6:05 PM
Typed 7:45 PM

MEMORANDUM FOR THE DIRECTOR

Re: JOHN STEINBECK - AUTHOR-

ALL INFORMATION CONTAINED
HEREIN IS UNCLASSIFIED
EXCEPT WHERE SHOWN
OTHERWISE

173

In response to her previous request I telephonically advised Miss Collins in the Attorney General's office that we had in our possession two pamphlets which concerned the above-entitled individual. One of these entitled "Their Blood Is Strong" was written by the subject and published in 1938 by the Simon J. Lubin Society of California. The material in this pamphlet is similar to that contained in his book "The Grapes of Wrath" and concerns the activities of migratory agricultural workers. The other pamphlet, which was furnished to us in May, 1938, is entitled "Writers Take Sides" and contains the opinions of several hundred authors as to whether they are for or against Franco. I informed Miss Collins that the subject was one of the authors quoted therein and further advised her I would make these pamphlets available to her for whatever purpose she may need them. Miss Collins stated she would appreciate the use of them very much.

Respectfully,

Edward A. Tamm

RECORDED
INDEXED

100-106224-5

15 NOV 8 1942

58 NOV 18 1942

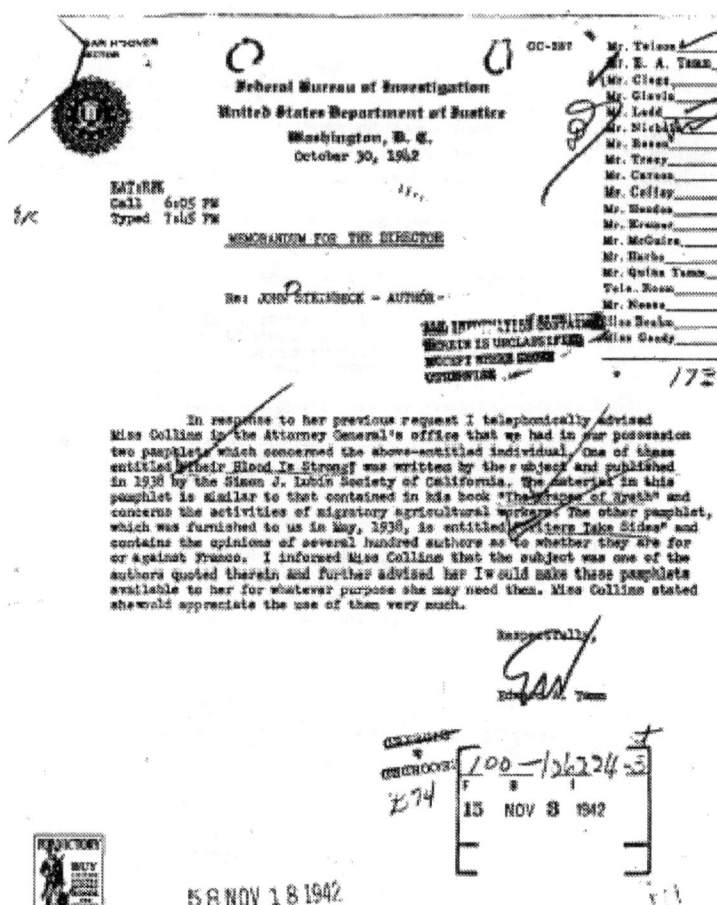

West Palm Be(),Florida.

December 5,1942.

Hon. J.Edgar Hoover,
Chief of F.B.I.Washington,D.C.

Subject: JOHN ERNST STEINBECK
Complaint: Proposed agitation of Japanese Relocation Centers, California & West.

Sir:--

For some time past I have resented books by Steinbeck, for they portray such unrepresentative pictures of our American life in rural districts. I live near the Everglades farms district and most of the migrants out there live better than I do, while they are here for the picking season.

46578

Steinbeck's name is John Ernst Steinbeck. His father was a German, born in Florida of German parents, according to the story in WHO'S WHO in U.S. writing circles. But of course the author furnishes the information about himself.

My reason for writing this is that it is rumored that Steinbeck is now gathering information for a heart-throb about the sad condition of Japanese in Relocation Centers in the West. I think it would be best for all concerned that he be not permitted to issue such a story until after the war— if ever.

Under strict enforcement of postal regulations, Steinbeck's books would not be permitted to go through U.S. mails, because of their scurrilous and obscene passages. These are held up as examples of the immoral life of the U.S. in foreign countries opposed to us. I understand his books have been translated into German and circulated as "horrible examples," but I cannot prove this.

THIS LETTER DOES NOT NEED A REPLY.
IT IS ONLY SENT TO YOU. . . . . AS INFORMATION.

You may have all this information from other sources; but I will explain why I am writing it. During the other World War I made reports direct to [redacted] when they did not concern local matters, but came to my attention regarding other sections of the country. I had authority to do this.

Where is Mr. Steinbeck?
Is he attempting to get information concerning government housing of soldiers?

He might dress in uniform and hang around incomplete camps like Boca Ratone, trying to get information as to inadequacy of camps before they are completed and outfitted perfectly. I hope this will not occur.

RECORDED & INDEXED

Respectfully yours [redacted]

Mail address [redacted]

100-106224-3X

"H-13"
EX-5

JOHN STEINBECK

b7C

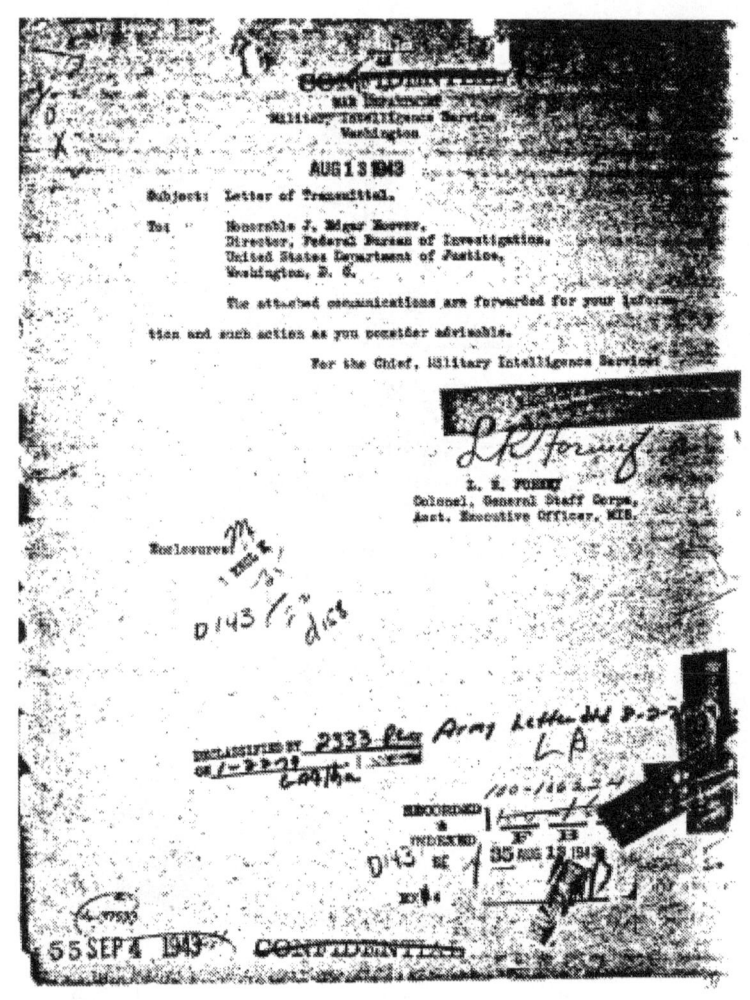

CONFIDENTIAL

WAR DEPARTMENT
Military Intelligence Service
Washington

AUG 13 1943

Subject: Letter of Transmittal.

To: Honorable J. Edgar Hoover,
Director, Federal Bureau of Investigation,
United States Department of Justice,
Washington, D. C.

The attached communications are forwarded for your information and such action as you consider advisable.

For the Chief, Military Intelligence Service:

[redacted]

L. R. Forney

L. R. FORNEY
Colonel, General Staff Corps,
Asst. Executive Officer, MIS.

Enclosures:

D143

DECLASSIFIED BY 2333
ON 1-2-79

Army letter dtd

LA

100-146

RECORDED & INDEXED

F B

35 AUG 19 1943

D143

55 SEP 4 1943

CONFIDENTIAL

Headquarters Western Defense Command and 4th Army
ACofS, G-2, Presidio of San Francisco, California -

II-C/S-11305c   27 July 1943

SUBJECT: John E. STEINBECK, 15041 De Cado Drive, Sherman Oaks, California

TO : Chief, MIS, War Department, Washington, D. C.

1. Attention is invited to our CI-R1 report dated 27 January 1943, Subject as above, representing investigation conducted in the vicinity of Los Angeles, California, and memorandum report dated 25 April 1943, Subject as above, covering investigation conducted in the Second Service Command previously forwarded your office.

2. Enclosed find CI-R1 report dated 13 July 1943 representing investigation conducted in the vicinity of San Francisco, California.

3. This office does not concur in the recommendations by the reporting agent in closing report. In view of substantial doubt as to Subject's loyalty and discretion, it is recommended that Subject not be considered favorably for a commission in the Army of the United States.

4. Undeveloped leads will not be followed in the absence of request, and this case is considered closed in this office.

For the AC of S, G-2:

BORIS T. PASH
Lt. Col., M.I.
Chief, Counter Intelligence Branch

1 Incl: (in trip)
CI-R1 dtd 7-13-43

MID dist: WSH.

100-106224-3X1

DECLASSIFIED BY 3333 per Army letter dtd 8-2-78

WAR DEPARTMENT — CONFIDENTIAL

MILITARY INTELLIGENCE DIVISION

File No. [illegible]
Date: 13 July, 1942
Subject:

JOHN E. STEINBECK
[illegible] Del Mar Drive
Sherman Oaks, California

Investigation requested by: [illegible], San Francisco, Calif.
Office of origin: A C of S, G-2, [illegible] & 4th Army
Report made at: San Francisco, California
Report made by: [illegible]
Period covered: [illegible] 1942 to [illegible] July, 1942
Character of investigation: [illegible]
Status of Case: CLOSED

REASON FOR INVESTIGATION:

By letter dated 16 February, 1942, from the A C of S, G-2, [illegible] and Fourth Army, Presidio of San Francisco, California, to the [illegible] Branch Office, G-2, [illegible] and Fourth Army, San Francisco, California, it was requested that a proper investigation be made in this area to determine the discretion, integrity and loyalty of Subject, and his suitability to hold a commission in the army of the United States.

DETAILS:

[illegible]: This [illegible] supplements previous report prepared at Los Angeles, California, under date of 27 January, 1942, made by Special Agent [illegible] Johnson, CIC, Los Angeles, California.

1. Personal Data:

Birth:	27 February, 1902, Salinas, California.
Present Age:	41 years
Description:	Height 6' [illegible]; weight [illegible] lbs.
Characteristics:	Loyal, honest, sincere, [illegible] author, [illegible], sensitive nature. ([illegible])
Marital Status:	Received interlocutory decree of divorce 13 March, 1942.

2. Family Data:

Father, John Ernest Steinbeck (deceased), born in St. Augustine, Florida.
Mother, Olive [illegible] Steinbeck (deceased), born in Salinas, California.
Sister: Mrs. [illegible], [illegible], California.
Wife, Carol Steinbeck, interlocutory decree of divorce, 13 March, 1942

Continued on Page

Forwarded,
MID, Washington, D. C. — 2 copies
~~HQ, Los Angeles Office~~ — 1 copies
~~Procurement District~~ — copies
~~[illegible]~~ — copies

Reviewed and Approved:
For the AC of S, G-2:

RICHARD C. [illegible]
Major, Inf.
Chief, [illegible] Sub-Section
Counter Intelligence Branch

~~CONFIDENTIAL~~

WAR DEPARTMENT
[illegible]

Incl #1

23

CONFIDENTIAL

[illegible] [illegible]
JOHN E. STEINBECK

3. Education: [illegible] - 1919, Salinas Union School, graduated; 3 years at Leland Stanford University; majored in journalism; did not graduate.

4. Employment: At present working for self as an author; has sold [illegible] stories to the Motion Picture Industry.
March 194[illegible] to December 194[illegible], employed as Special Consultant to the Secretary of War, assigned to the Commanding General, Army Air Forces. Made an exhaustive study of flying and training, and now writing an official book on this subject. No salary.
December 194[illegible] to March 194[illegible], employed by the Office of War Information, 270 Madison Avenue, New York City, as a Foreign News editor at a salary of $[illegible] per year.

Also Vice-President of the Pacific Biological Laboratories, Inc., for a number of years where he helped to operate a commercial laboratory.

5. Military History: None

6. [illegible] and Office Check: None

7. Addresses: 1942 to present, 15041 Del Gado Drive, Sherman Oaks, Calif.
December, 1941 to March, 1942, New York City, New York.
July, 1936 to December, 1941, Los Gatos, California.
Subject has lived most of his life near Salinas and Carmel, California, except for the time spent in Los Gatos and on intermittent trips to Los Angeles, New York City, and other parts of the world. (Name [illegible])

8. Residence Check:

Mr. Hugh Porter, 344 California Street, San Francisco, California; purchaser of Subject's former residence at Los Gatos. (U) Name [illegible]
Mr. F. [illegible], neighbor of Subject at Los Gatos, California. (U) Name [illegible]

9. Organizations:

Western Writers' Congress, 1936
Committee to Aid Agricultural Organization, 1938, (Name 1)
Schneiderman-Darcy Defense Committee, 1940 (Name 1)
Emergency Youth Assembly, 1937, (Name 1)

CONFIDENTIAL

Page 2

~~CONFIDENTIAL~~

[illegible]
JOHN E. STEINBECK

9. Organizations: (continued)

International Union of Revolutionary Writers of Moscow.
League of American Writers, [illegible].
National Institute of Arts and Letters, [illegible].

10. Principal Amusements: Marine Biology.

11. References: No references given in San Francisco, California area.

12. Acquaintances: Mr. Martin Ray, Saratoga, California. [illegible] (Name [illegible])
Miss Barbara [illegible], [illegible] Jackson Street, San Francisco, California. [illegible] (Name [illegible])
Mr. E.L. Roberts, Cashier, First National Bank, Los Gatos, California. [illegible] (Name [illegible])
Mr. Webster Street, of [illegible], Martin & Ferrante, California. [illegible] (Name [illegible])
Mrs. Carol Steinbeck, [illegible] Eardley Avenue, Pacific Grove, California. [illegible] (Name [illegible])

13. Credit Record: Satisfactory (Name [illegible])

14. Police Record: San Francisco Police Dept., NR (Name [illegible])
Federal Bureau of Investigation, San Francisco, NR (Name [illegible])
ONI, 12th Naval District, San Francisco, NR but ONI files refer to one, JOHN STEINBECK, PO Box [illegible], Los Gatos, Calif. as subscriber to PEOPLE'S WORLD as of Sept. 1939. (Name [illegible])
American Legion Radical Research Bureau, San Francisco, California show record of Subject from December [illegible], 193[illegible] through June 4, 1939. (Name [illegible])
Sheriff's Office, Santa Clara County, Calif. NR (Name [illegible])
Los Gatos Police Dept. NR (Name [illegible])
Salinas, California Police Dept. NR (Name [illegible])
Carmel Calif., Police Dept. NR (Name [illegible])
Monterey, Calif. Police Dept. NR (Name [illegible])

ADVERSE INFORMATION:

1. Subject has associated with individuals who are known to have a radical political and economic philosophy, and with some members of the Communist Party. (Names A, B, [illegible] and [illegible])

Page 3

~~CONFIDENTIAL~~

CONFIDENTIAL

LA [illegible]
JOHN E. STEINBECK

ADVERSE INFORMATION: (continued)

[illegible]. Subject received large volume of Communistic literature and possessed books expressing radical political and economic views, in his library. (Items [illegible])

5. Subject's former wife, Carol Steinbeck, registered as a Communist in Santa Clara County in 1938. (Items [illegible])

UNDEVELOPED LEADS: Request investigations as follows

A C of S, G-2, 2nd Service Command, Governors Island, New York

(1) Interview Subject's agents, McIntosh and Otis, 18 East 41st Street, New York City, to determine Subject's associations and activities in that vicinity. Such leads should be developed with particular attention to Communist associations and relations.

(2) To determine what relations has had with the League of American Writers by contacting the League's headquarters in New York City.

(3) To contact Major Moltmann, AAF, 30 Broad Street, New York City, who has made allegations that Subject is quite a heavy drinker and has communistic tendencies.

(4) Make an office and employment check at the office of War Information, 570 Madison Avenue, New York City, where Subject was employed from December 1941 to March, 1942.

A C of S, MIS, War Department, Washington, D.C.

(1) To make necessary office and employment check to determine Subject's employment as a Special Consultant to the Secretary of War, assigned to the Commanding General, Army Air Forces. Particular attention to be given to any possible Communist associations and connections.

(2) To check with FBI, ONI, MIS and Dies Committee files to determine any record extant on Subject. The Dies Committee should have a resume of Subject's activities written by Thomas Gerett forthe Los Angeles Office of the Dies Committee.

Page 6

CONFIDENTIAL

CONFIDENTIAL

SA- [illegible] IX-G/2 [illegible]
JOHN E. STEINBECK

REMARKS AND CONCLUSIONS:

This investigation revealed that Subject is honest, loyal, patriotic and an excellent and sincere writer. Although Subject exercised poor discretion during his early days of writing by associating with some elements of the Communist Party, he was not interested in advancing the cause of the Party but in gathering material for his writings on certain social conditions existing in this country at that time.

Subject wrote various articles which were published by Communist organizations because the economic views expressed were considered radical. However, Subject rejected communistic political and economic theories repeatedly and discarded his association with this element when it became apparent that his prestige was being used to further the interests of the Party.

Subject, in this Agent's opinion, possesses the requisites of honesty, loyalty and discretion necessary for a commission in the Army of the United States. Subject is sincere in his beliefs concerning the social and economic situation of the under classes in this country and in his desire to have their lot improved.

Subject is a candid and powerful writer.

RECOMMENDATIONS:

This Agent recommends that Subject be given a commission in the Army of the United States if he can be placed where his writing ability may be utilized.

G- 2 NOTE:

This office does not concur in the recommendations of the investigative agent, and believing that substantial doubt exists as to Subject's loyalty and discretion, recommends that Subject not be favorably considered for a commission in the Army of the United States. Undeveloped leads will not be followed in the absence of a request, and this case is considered closed in this office.

APPROVED:

T. M. FAIRCHILD
Lt. Colonel, MI
Officer in Charge

NB: Subj. previously disapproved for a Commission by War Dept. Personnel Board WAH

CONFIDENTIAL

Page 8

CONFIDENTIAL

Salinas, California
May 29, 1943
Case No. [illegible]

MEMORANDUM FOR THE OFFICER IN CHARGE

SUBJECT: JOHN E. STEINBECK
425 Eardley Avenue
Pacific Grove, California

RE: Covering Memorandum.

Three excellent sources of information — the former Postmaster, Subject's attorney, and Subject's [illegible] — agree on these points:

1. Subject is not a communist.

2. Subject is loyal, patriotic, honest.

3. Subject is an excellent writer.

4. Subject would make a good officer if his writing ability is utilized.

AGENT'S NOTES

This Agent believes that Subject would pass the requisite honesty, loyalty and integrity insofar as his commission in the United States Army is concerned. It is the question of whether Subject would be of more value as a civilian employee or as an officer that higher authorities must decide. If Subject is to be employed by the United States Army in positions in which his stark writing ability may be utilized, it is the opinion of this Agent that he should be commissioned.

[illegible]
Special Agent [illegible]

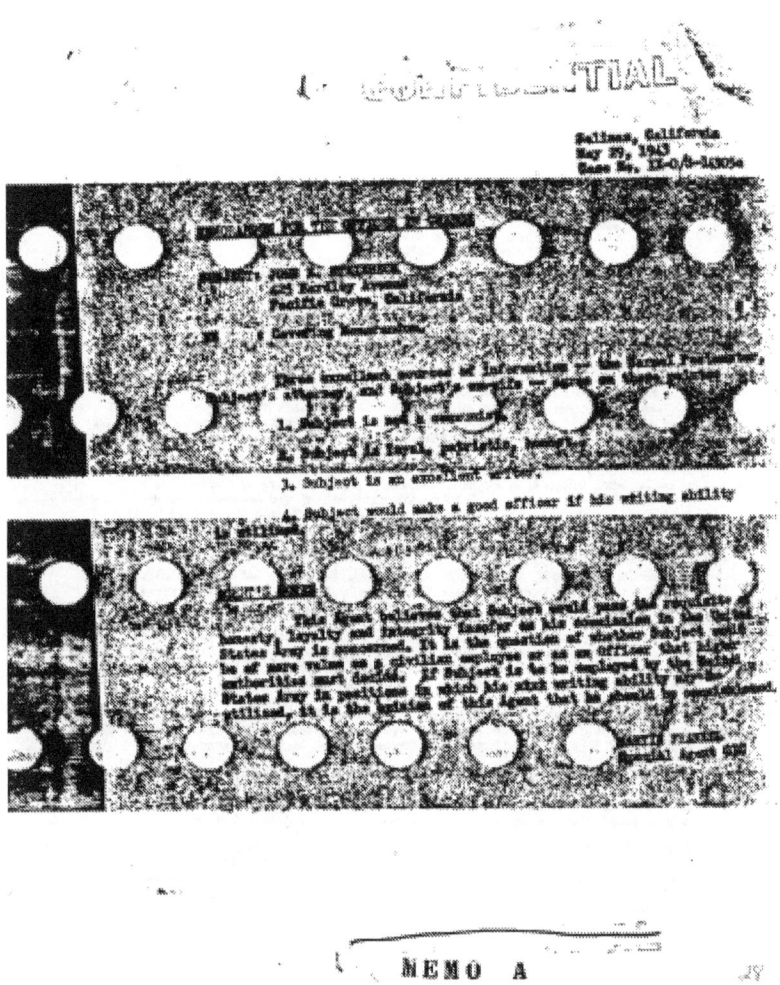

MEMO A

TOP SECRET

C O N F I D E N T I A L

San Francisco, California
30 June 1943
Case No. II-G/S-14305a

MEMORANDUM FOR THE OFFICER IN CHARGE

Subject: JOHN E. STEINBECK
15941 Del Gado Drive
Sherman Oaks, California

Re: Interview with Mr. MARTIN RAY, Acquaintance.

On June 9, 1943, this Agent interviewed Mr. MARTIN RAY, intimate acquaintance of Subject. RAY associated with STEINBECK and his former wife, CAROL STEINBECK, during the entire time Subject's residence was in Los Gatos, California. Informant is presently residing on Masson Road, Saratoga, California.

RAY believes Subject to be absolutely loyal to the government although Subject associated with some elements of the Communist Party in his earliest days of writing. Subject repeatedly stated to RAY that he was not a Communist but was interested in the lower-class working people regardless of their particular political creed. RAY explained that Subject had written certain articles for publications which were considered Communistic but that these articles were written to explain Subject's point of view of the social problem involved and not to further the interest of the Communist Party. Subject, according to RAY, gradually realized that he was being used by the Party and severed all connections with this element after his books began to have a wide sale.

CAROL STEINBECK, former wife of Subject, told RAY that she registered with the Communist Party in Santa Clara County in 1938 simply to observe the local reaction and that Subject was strongly opposed to this act.

Following the sale of one of Subject's earlier books, Subject and his wife made a trip to Europe, visiting Sweden and Russia. RAY stated that Subject was deeply impressed by the economic and political policies of Sweden but was not impressed, nor did he discuss, the government of Russia.

Concerning Subject's character, RAY stated Subject's integrity was beyond question. Subject is very sensitive and sentimental; is deeply devoted to his friends and is easily influenced by these friends to grant large favors.

RAY believes Subject should be commissioned in the Army only if Subject's writing ability may be efficiently utilized. According to RAY, Subject would work very hard writing for the benefit of his country but is not qualified to hold a commission in any other situation.

Agent's Notes:
RAY is a close friend of Subject and has tremendous respect for Subject's writing ability. This Agent believes RAY is interested in Subject's welfare as a friend yet was absolutely fair and impartial in his recollections of Subject and Subject's suitability for a commission in the Army.

EMO B

CHARLES O. SHIELDS
Agent, CIC

C O N F I D E N T I A L

CONFIDENTIAL

San Francisco, California
June 14, 1943
Case No. IX-C/S-14806a

MEMORANDUM FOR THE OFFICER IN CHARGE

SUBJECT: JOHN E. STEINBECK
15041 Del Gado Drive
Sherman Oaks, California

RE: Acquaintance check with Miss Barbara Burke

On June 9, 1943, this Agent interviewed MISS BARBARA BURKE, 3048 Jackson Street, San Francisco, California regarding Subject.

MISS BURKE bought the Subject's first house at Los Gatos and became intimately acquainted as the Subject lived on the premises for a short time thereafter. MISS BURKE believes Subject to be unquestionably loyal, having heard him say that he had never voted the communistic ticket, and was strongly opposed to his wife's registration with the party. MISS BURKE further stated that Subject had always voted Democratic tickets, and was heartily in favor of the policies of the New Deal.

MISS BURKE stated Subject is a very heavy drinker, but she had never seen him intoxicated. Subject's political philosophy, MISS BURKE considered to be merely "leftish" in the social changes calculated to improve the conditions of the working classes, and felt Subject's integrity to be unimpeachable.

Agent's notes: Informant has the greatest respect for the literary work of Subject, but appeared to this Agent to be sincere and candid in her description of Subject's qualities.

CHARLES O. SHIELDS
Agent, CIC

CONFIDENTIAL

MEMO C

TOP SECRET

~~CONFIDENTIAL~~

San Francisco, California
June 14, 1943
Case No. [illegible]

MEMORANDUM FOR THE OFFICER IN CHARGE

SUBJECT: JOHN E. STEINBECK
13041 Del Gado Drive
Sherman Oaks, California

RE: Residence check

On June 8, 1943, this Agent interviewed MR. HUGH PORTER, 244 California Street, San Francisco, California, purchaser of Subject's house in Los Gatos.

MR. PORTER did not know Subject personally, but had Subject's belongings moved from the house. He stated that Subject's second-class mail was tremendous, much of it apparently communistic. MR. PORTER read various parts at random and found it very radical. Subject's library, left in the former residence, contained many radical books.

Informant's opinion of Subject based upon observation of conditions under which Subject lived is that Subject is very impulsive, eccentric, and unreliable socially. Informant had no knowledge of Subject's economical or political views except from the circumstantial evidence stated above.

MR. PORTER stated that Subject employed a Japanese house boy, Joe Higashi, who continued to work after Subject left. HIGASHI had books, ostensibly propaganda containing pictures of Axis leaders and accomplishments. HIGASHI is now evacuated to the interior.

Agent's notes: PORTER did not know Subject, but is very much opposed to economic and political views of Subject as indicated by type of mail received and contents of Subject's library.

Agent, CIC

~~CONFIDENTIAL~~

[redacted]

San Francisco, California
30 June 1943
Case No. II-C/S-14309a

MEMORANDUM FOR THE OFFICER IN CHARGE

Subject: JOHN E. STEINBECK
15041 Del Gado Drive
Sherman Oaks, California

Re: Residence Check.

On June 8, 1943, this Agent interviewed Mr. F. RAINERI, Los Gatos, California, neighbor of Subject, during the time Subject resided in Los Gatos.

Informant stated that Subject was friendly but generally very aloof. Subject, according to RAINERI, apparently made frequent visits out of town while living in Los Gatos. RAINERI recalled no derogatory remarks concerning Subject; however, informant had heard that Subject was very sensitive and desired to be avoided by the local people so that he could concentrate on his writing without interruption.

Agent's Note:

This neighbor lived approximately one-half mile from Subject and had little in common with Subject.

CHARLES G. [illegible]
Agent, CIC

~~CONFIDENTIAL~~

32

[redacted]

San Francisco, California
June 11, 1942
Case No. II-G/S-[illegible]

MEMORANDUM FOR THE OFFICER IN CHARGE

SUBJECT: JOHN E. STEINBECK
15041 Del Gado Drive
Sherman Oaks, California

RE: Acquaintance check

On June 8, 1942, this Agent interviewed MR. H. E. L. ROBERTS, cashier First National Bank, Los Gatos, California.

Subject had an account in the bank from July 1, 1936 to June 20, 1941. ROBERTS impression of Subject was that he is very quiet and reserved. Subject usually is very poorly dressed.

Agent's notes: ROBERTS had no knowledge of Subject's economical or political views, and had not heard any derogatory remarks concerning his loyalty or integrity.

CHARLES C. [illegible]
Agent, CIC

C-O-N-F-I-D-E-N-T-I-A-L

MEMO F

CONFI[illegible]TIAL

Salinas, California
May 26, 1943
Case No. [illegible]

[illegible]

SUBJECT: JOHN E. [illegible]
[illegible] Avenue
Pacific Grove, California

RE [illegible]

On May [illegible], 1943 this Agent interviewed [illegible], of [illegible] & [illegible], attorneys, Monterey, California, in connection with the investigation of Subject, who has applied for a commission in the United States Army.

[illegible] said that he [illegible] Subject's attorney, [illegible] Subject since 192[illegible], and would classify him as a generous, large, [illegible] [illegible], and [illegible].

According to [illegible], Subject's legal and permanent address is [illegible] AVENUE, PACIFIC GROVE, CALIFORNIA. Other addresses are temporary, dependent upon the current locale of his work. His personal effects and furniture are at the Pacific Grove address, and this home is used for legal and tax purposes. Subject, said [illegible], was finally divorced from [illegible] STEINBECK in March, 1943, remarried, to [illegible] STEINBECK, with whom he lived after this marriage in New York City. Subject has a sister in Carmel, another in Watsonville, another in Berkeley, all California cities. The husband of the the sister residing in Carmel is a Lt. Colonel in Africa, attached to the Transport Service, U.S. Army. [illegible]

Subject's former wife CAROL, stated [illegible], lives in Carmel, California. CAROL STEINBECK, against her husband's wishes, registered as a communist. This action reflected unfavorably against her husband.

Subject's father, continued [illegible], had been a [illegible] of Monterey County, California for fifteen years. His mother was a well known [illegible] in Salinas, California.

[illegible] said he had received a letter from Subject, May [illegible], 1943, in which Subject stated he was leaving for England very shortly as a correspondent and special writer of the New York HERALD TRIBUNE.

[illegible] was positive Subject was a not a communist, had no communist leanings, that his honesty, loyalty and integrity were of the best, that he was intensely patriotic, and would make an excellent officer if able to use his writing talent.

AGENT'S NOTE

Informant, and his law firm, have a reputation in Monterey for conservation.

MARTIN FRANKEL
Special Agent [illegible]

CONFIDENTIAL

Salinas, California
May 26, 1943
Case No. [illegible]

MEMORANDUM FOR THE OFFICER IN CHARGE

SUBJECT: JOHN E. STEINBECK
[illegible] Eardley Avenue
Pacific Grove, California
[illegible]

On May 26, 1943 this Agent interviewed FREDERICK [illegible], [illegible], Carmel, California, in connection with the investigation of Subject, who has applied for a Commission in the United States Army.

[illegible] stated as follows:

1. Subject's wife worked, in 193[illegible], on a WPA sewing project so that her husband, Subject, could continue writing. At this time he was getting material for GRAPES OF WRATH. Wife referred to was his first wife, CAROL [illegible], now a resident of Carmel, California.
2. [illegible] said he was well acquainted with Subject in his earlier writing days, around [illegible].
3. Subject associated with communists and radicals only to get material for his writings.
4. Subject is not a communist. He believed that the communist and Associated Farmers were both exploiting the migratory workers.
5. Subject will associate with anyone or any groups who will furnish material for his writing.
6. Subject is an excellent writer.
7. Subject's association with the communists is selfish — to learn about them so he can write about them.
8. Subject would make a good officer if he can use his writing talent.
9. Subject understands the leftist element and [illegible] stand for subversive [illegible] writings.
10. Subject is fundamentally a good citizen.
11. Subject is more genuine in his [illegible] than a lot of people who call themselves conservative.
12. If Subject had been of draft age he would not have tried in any way to avoid the draft; he would have gladly entered the army, trying to procure more material to use in his writings.
13. Subject's loyalty, honesty and integrity is of the highest.

AGENT'S NOTES:
[illegible] appeared to be very sincere, and attempting to offer fact as well as opinion.

MARTIN FRANKEL
Special Agent CIC

CONFIDENTIAL

MEMO B

CONFIDENTIAL

Salinas, California
May 28, 1943
Case No. II-O/S-14305a

MEMORANDUM FOR THE OFFICER IN CHARGE

SUBJECT: JOHN E. STEINBECK
[illegible]
Pacific Grove, California

RE: [illegible] [illegible] Acquaintance Check.

On May 28, 1943 this Agent interviewed Mrs. CAROL STEINBECK, Carmel, California, in connection with the investigation of Subject, who has applied for a commission in the United States Army.

CAROL STEINBECK stated that Subject does not have any fixed political beliefs, that he is a registered Democrat, and probably, on a broad basis, favors the New Deal.

CAROL STEINBECK said Subject got all his material for the GRAPES OF WRATH from the Farm Security Administration. His writings, according to informant, come before everything else in his life, and writing has been his passion since childhood.

CAROL STEINBECK said that Subject is not and never has been a member of the communist party, or even a sympathizer. She said that she had once registered as a Communist to see what would happen and what the reaction would be in a small town. Now she regrets this move because it caused comment that reflected upon Subject.

According to CAROL STEINBECK, Subject would make an excellent officer of the United States Army if he was assigned to duties wherein he could use his talent for writing. He is loyal, she asserted, honest and his integrity cannot be questioned.

AGENT'S NOTES

Subject was divorced from CAROL STEINBECK March, 19[illegible], and final March, 1943. Subject has remarried. Informant appeared to be sincere but did not give Subject the benefit of any doubts. She did not volunteer a great deal of information, and seemed to feel much resentful at the mention of Subject's name.

MARTIN FRANKEL
Special Agent CIC

MEMO I

TOP SECRET

C O N F I D E N T I A L

San Francisco, California
June 11, 1943
Case No. I E-0/S-14508e

MEMORANDUM FOR THE OFFICER IN CHARGE

SUBJECT: JOHN E. STEINBECK
15041 Del Gado Drive
Sherman Oaks, California

RE: Check of Voter's Registration
Files Santa Clara County, Calif.

On 9 June 1943 this Agent check the Voter's Registration files Santa Clara County, California to secure information concerning the Subject, who is being considered for a commission in the Army of the United States.

Registration files show that Subject's former wife, CAROL STEINBECK, registered as a Communist in Santa Clara County, 8 November 1938. On 16 September 1939, approximately one year later, Subject's wife registered in Santa Clara County as a Democrat. On the 13 June 1942, CAROL STEINBECK transferred her voting registration to Monterey, California.

No record was found of Subject having registered at any time as a Communist in Santa Clara County.

CHARLES O. SHIELDS
Agent, C I C

~~C O N F I D E N T I A L~~

MEMO J

87

CONFIDENTIAL

San Francisco, California
13 July 1943
Case No. [illegible]

MEMORANDUM FOR THE OFFICER IN CHARGE

Subject: JOHN E. STEINBECK
[illegible] Drive
Sherman Oaks, California

Re: Credit Check

On 13 July 1943 this Agent checked the records of the Retail Credit Association, 185 Stockton Street, San Francisco, California regarding the Subject. These records include reports from the Retail Merchant's Association of San Jose, California covering Santa Clara County.

The credit records indicate that the Subject enjoyed an excellent rating in 1940, had very good commercial and savings accounts in various California banks. Subject's income stated to be solely from writings and sale of stories to the motion picture industry.

CHARLES C. SHIELDS
Agent, CIC

CONFIDENTIAL

MEMO K

San Francisco, California,
May 1, 1942,
Case No. [illegible]-C/S-[illegible].

MEMORANDUM FOR THE OFFICER IN CHARGE

Subject: JOHN E. STEINBECK, aka Dr. [illegible],
[illegible] Del Gado Drive,
Sherman Oaks, California.

Re: Police check.

On February 23, 1942, this Agent checked the records of the Office of Naval Intelligence, 12th Naval District, the American Legion Radical Research Bureau, the San Francisco Field Office of the Federal Bureau of Investigation, and the San Francisco Police Department, all of San Francisco, California, regarding Subject.

The Federal Bureau of Investigation and the San Francisco Police Department reported no record of Subject.

The Office of Naval Intelligence reported the following record:

"ONI files refer to one John STEINBECK, P. O. Box [illegible], Los Gatos, Calif., who was a subscriber to the PEOPLE'S WORLD as of Sept., 1938. (It should be noted that John STEINBECK, the author, also maintained a home in Los Gatos)"

The American Legion Radical Research Bureau reported the following:

11/[illegible]-1935: Was Pacific Weekly contributor. Red publication at Carmel.
11/18-1936: One of the sponsors of the Assembly of Youth, January 9 and 10.
4/1-1936: Contributed article in this issue of Pacific Weekly (Red publication) re: The Racial Prejudice Among the Agricultural Workers in California.
10/17: Chairman of the newly formed Committee to Aid Agricultural Organization. (Very Red outfit).
8/[illegible]-1939: His book "The Grapes of Wrath" was branded as Red propaganda by Father A. D. Spearman, S.J., director of the library of Loyola, U.L.A.

His former wife, Carol [illegible] Steinbeck, was registered Communist, Santa Clara County – 1938 – while living at Rt. 1, Box [illegible], Los Gatos.

NICHOLAS [illegible],
Special Agent, CIC.

kf

MEMO L

CONFIDENTIAL

San Francisco, California
11 June 1943
Case No. IX-G/B-14805a

MEMORANDUM FOR THE OFFICER IN CHARGE

SUBJECT: JOHN E. STEINBECK
15041 Del Gado Drive
Sherman Oaks, California

RE: Police Check

On 8 June 1943 this Agent checked the records of the Sheriff's office, Santa Clara County, California and the Police Department, Los Gatos, California, regarding the Subject.

Police Department, Los Gatos . . . No Record.

Sheriff's Office, Santa Clara County . . . No Record.

CHARLES G. SHIELDS
Agent, CIC

~~CONFIDENTIAL~~

MEMO N

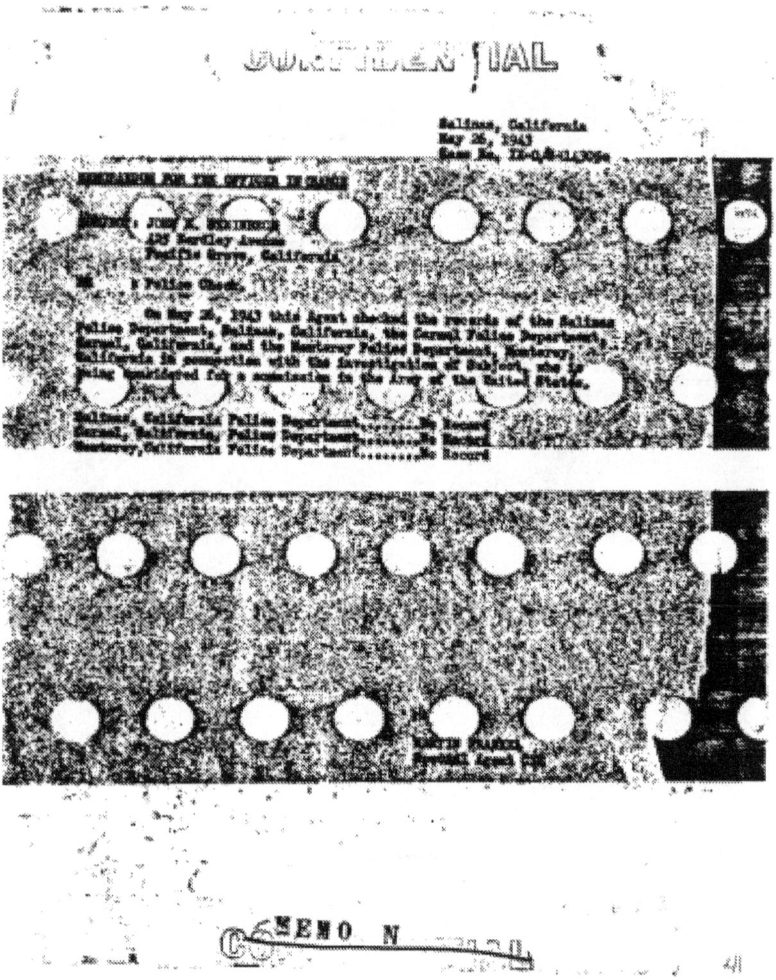

CONFIDENTIAL

Salinas, California
May 26, 1943
Case No. [illegible]

MEMORANDUM FOR THE OFFICER IN CHARGE

SUBJECT: JOHN E. STEINBECK
425 Eardley Avenue
Pacific Grove, California

RE: Police Check.

On May 26, 1943 this Agent checked the records of the Salinas Police Department, Salinas, California, the Carmel Police Department, Carmel, California, and the Monterey Police Department, Monterey, California in connection with the investigation of Subject, who is being considered for a commission in the Army of the United States.

Salinas, California Police Department..........No Record
Carmel, California, Police Department..........No Record
Monterey, California Police Department..........No Record

[illegible]
Special Agent [illegible]

MEMO N

CONFIDENTIAL

Office Memorandum • UNITED STATES GOVERNMENT

TO : Director, FBI DATE: April 8, 1944

FROM : SAC, San Antonio

SUBJECT: JOHN ERNST STEINBECK
Incoming Passenger, Brownsville, Texas
3/15/44
FOREIGN TRAVEL CONTROL

ALL INFORMATION CONTAINED
HEREIN IS UNCLASSIFIED
EXCEPT WHERE SHOWN
OTHERWISE

Reference is made to Bureau memorandum to San Antonio dated March 21, 1944, in the above-captioned matter. For the information of the New York City Office, reference memorandum advised that an investigation was conducted by Military Intelligence Division concerning the above-captioned individual to determine his loyalty and suitability to hold a commission in the Army of the United States, and that information had been received by the Bureau indicating that in view of substantial doubt as to the loyalty and discretion of the subject, a recommendation was made that he should not be considered favorably for a Commission in the U. S. Army.

This is to advise that on March 15, 1944, the subject, accompanied by his wife, GWIN CONGER STEINBECK, entered Brownsville, Texas, via Pan American Clipper enroute from the Reforma Hotel, Mexico, D. F. to their residence at 330 E. 51st Street, New York City. At the time of their entry, it was ascertained that the subject was an American citizen born at Salinas, California, on February 27, 1902, and that his wife was also an American citizen, having been born in Chicago, Illinois, October 25, 1918. It was also learned that the subject is presently employed as a writer by the New York Herald Tribune and that in 1943 he had been on a six-months assignment to England, Africa, and Sicily as a war correspondent.

The subject advised that on that assignment he had been slightly wounded and that the purpose of his present two-months trip to Mexico City had been to regain his health before resuming his work for the above-mentioned newspaper.

The above is being submitted for the information of the Bureau and a copy of this letter has been designated for the information of the New York City Office. No further action in this matter is presently contemplated by this Office.

DECLASSIFIED BY 2333 Pem Army letter dtd 8-2-78
ON 1-29-79

RRM:dam

CC New York City

100-106224-4X

RECORDED & INDEXED

APR 15 1944

APPROPRIATE AGENCIES AND FIELD OFFICES ADVISED BY ROUTING SLIP(S) OF
DATE

APR 24 1944

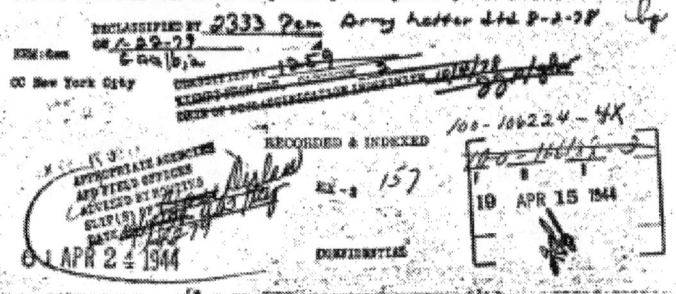

CONFIDENTIAL

Jan 18, 1947

Hon. J. Edgar hoover
Washington, D. C.

Dear Sir:

I trust that your agents in San Francisco are watching these series of alticles with much interest.

No doubt you have a file on this John Steinbeck; one of our foremost Commie inspired writers who had written many stories whose theme was to stir up class conciousness. Grapes of Wrath etc.

The most shocking element here is the fact that Steinbeck is even given space on the San Francisco, after being denouced by W. R. Hearst bac in 38 or 39. As you know doubt know, [redacted] blasted this picture Grapes of Wrath , seeing the underlying motives.

The very same executives on this paper purged this girl for her consta attack on the Commie themes emmanating from Hollywood.

I wrote a letter to [redacted] of the Los Angeles Examiner , regading this Steinbeck, seeking to hold up the articles. Also asking just who was responsible for this right about face . it seems that this is the only Hearst sheet that is carring Steinbeck's series.

How can Steinbeck have such "easy access to "INSIDE THE IRON CURTAIN" when YOU and other LOYAL Americans are forbibben to enter .

San Francisco is a veritable LITTLE MOSCOW to be sure.

I fully realize that the Examiner came out "finally" for the new local Mayor Robinson, who ran on an Anti Commie platform. But the paper finally entered the picture after Robinson had a commanding lead. Merely stating that they were Robinson because they figured he would win. NOT because he was the best ...

100-106224-5

mind you or the principles that he stood for..

When I arrived here a year ago , I proceeded to inform Robinson of Frank Havenner's record in Washington, which had been kept very much in the dark on the West Coast. With all this information it was clear sailing to be sure. This RED minority element in San Francisco is plentyb dangerous , and a verit paper keg. Of course I appreciate the fact that I am not telling you any thi that is new.

This Steinbeck running in the Examiner over Ada's dead body, a girl who was willing to sacrifice her very life for her country stands vindicate today for the fight she had even within her own ranks on this paper.

b7c I expected [redacted] to bring this matter to Mr. Hearst's attention, who is residing as you know ,in Beverly Hills..

I trust that this information will prove to be helpful to you.

With kindest regards ,

Yours most/sincerely,

b7c [redacted]

San Simeon, Calif..

A Russian Journal—

Amateur Play; A Club Dance

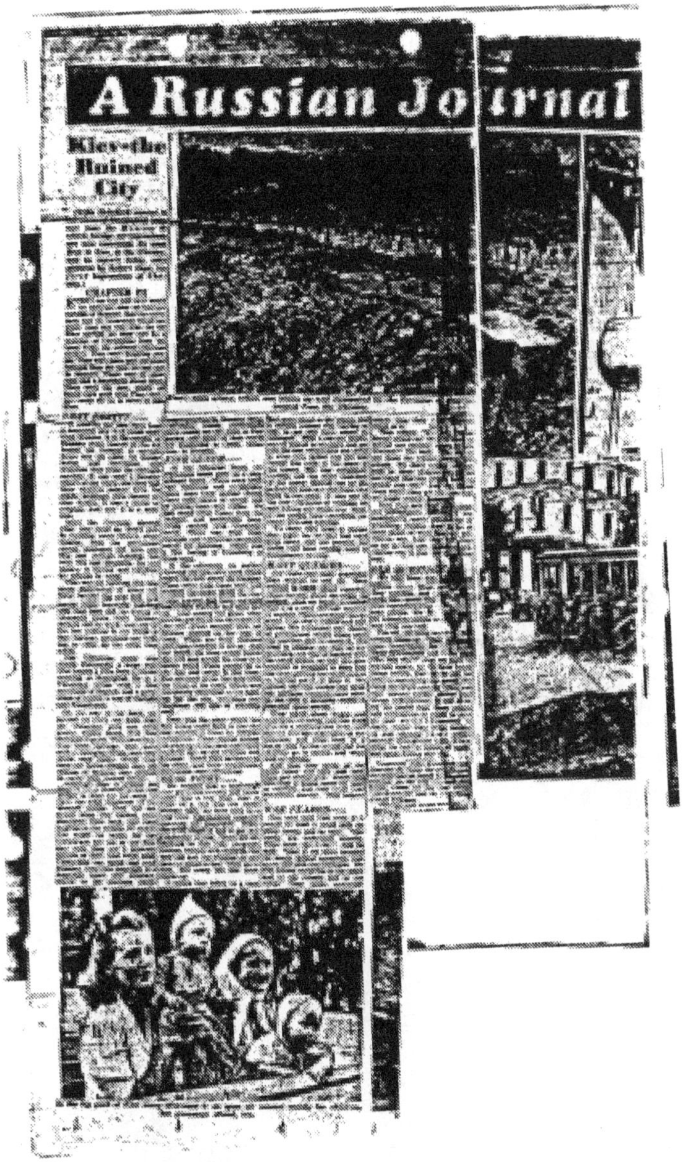

A Russian Jo[u]rnal

Kiev—the Ruined City

ALL INFORMATION CONTAINED
HEREIN IS UNCLASSIFIED
EXCEPT WHERE SHOWN
OTHERWISE

March 18, 1952

46576

JOHN ERNEST STEINBECK

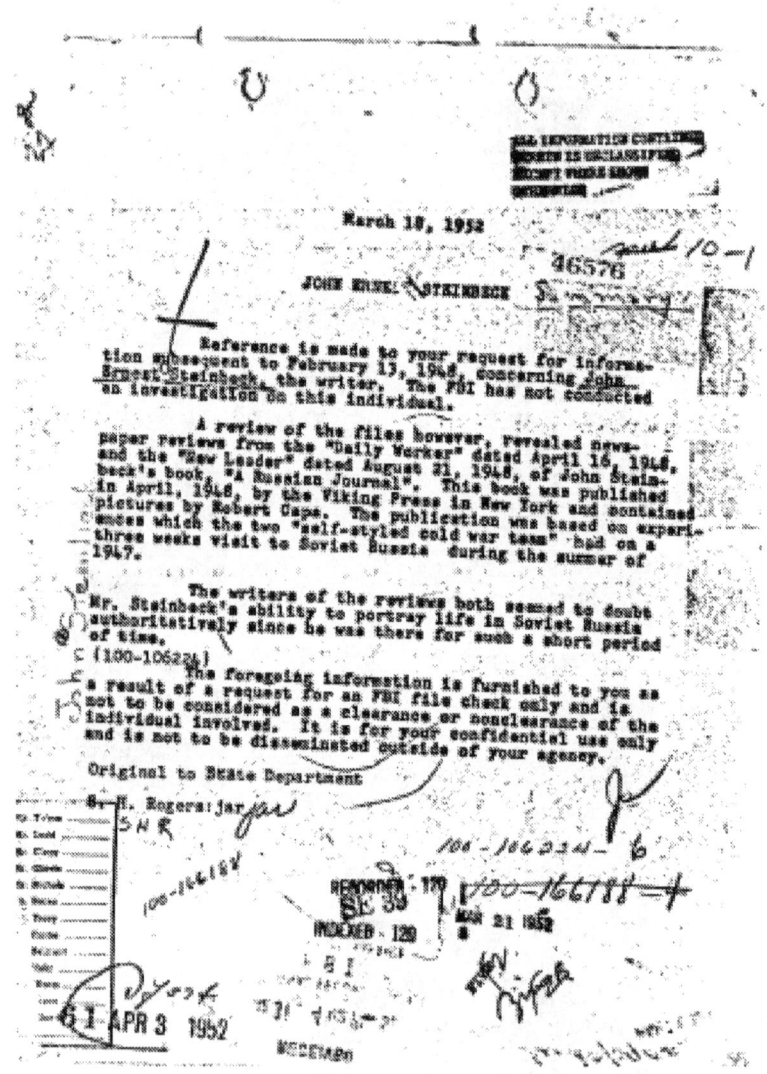

Reference is made to your request for information subsequent to February 13, 1948, concerning John
Ernest Steinbeck, the writer. The FBI has not conducted
an investigation on this individual.

A review of the files however, revealed newspaper reviews from the "Daily Worker" dated April 16, 1948,
and the "New Leader" dated August 21, 1948, of John Steinbeck's book, "A Russian Journal". This book was published
in April, 1948, by the Viking Press in New York and contained
pictures by Robert Capa. The publication was based on experiences which the two "self-styled cold war team" had on a
three weeks visit to Soviet Russia during the summer of
1947.

The writers of the reviews both seemed to doubt
Mr. Steinbeck's ability to portray life in Soviet Russia
authoritatively since he was there for such a short period
of time.

(100-106224)

The foregoing information is furnished to you as
a result of a request for an FBI file check only and is
not to be considered as a clearance or nonclearance of the
individual involved. It is for your confidential use only
and is not to be disseminated outside of your agency.

Original to State Department

S. H. Rogers:jar

100-106224-6

RECORDED - 170

SE 33

INDEXED - 120

MAR 21 1952

61 APR 3 1952

RECEIVED

March 10, 1954

ALL INFORMATION CONTAINED HEREIN IS UNCLASSIFIED EXCEPT WHERE SHOWN OTHERWISE

JOHN ERNST STEINBECK 46575

BIOGRAPHICAL DATA:

John Ernest Steinbeck, author, playwright and war correspondent, was born at Salinas, California, on February 27, 1902. He graduated from Salinas High School in 1919 and was a student at Stanford University for five years but did not graduate. He married Carol Henning in 1930 and was divorced from her in March, 1943. He married Gwyn Conger on March 29, 1943, and Elaine Scott on December 28, 1950. He has been the author of a number of books and was awarded the Pulitzer prize in 1940. Among the books for which he is most noted are "Tortilla Flat," 1935; "Of Mice And Men," 1937; "Grapes Of Wrath," 1939; "The Moon Is Down," 1942; "Cannery Row," 1945; "The Wayward Bus," 1947; and "A Russian Journal," 1948. He was also employed as a war correspondent and as a writer for the "New York Herald Tribune" during 1943, 1944, 1947, and 1948. Steinbeck was Vice President of World Video, Inc., an organization chartered in New York State on December 19, 1947, for the purpose of preparing television programs. ("Who's Who In America," 1952-53; 100-106188-2, [redacted] 100-340922-111, p. 1, 23)

b7d

CLASSIFIED BY 1259

EXEMPT FROM GDS, [illegible] 2, 3

DATE OF DECLASSIFICATION INDEFINITE

BUREAU INVESTIGATION:

The Bureau has conducted no investigation concerning John Steinbeck. However, under date of May 11, 1942, Attorney General Biddle forwarded to the Bureau a letter received by him from Steinbeck which stated in part "Do you suppose you could ask Edgar's boys to stop stepping on my heels? They think I am an enemy alien. It's getting tiresome." After checking the Bureau files the Attorney General was advised that Steinbeck was not being and never had been investigated. (100-106224-1)

INVESTIGATION BY G-2:

Steinbeck was investigated by G-2 during 1943 to determine his suitability to hold a commission in the U. S. Army. After investigation the Chief, Counter Intelligence Branch, G-2, recommended he not be considered favorably for

INDEXED - 29

EX. - 107

NOT RECORDED

138 MAR 20 1954

Per Army letter

a commission. Investigation developed that Steinbeck's former wife, Carol, had registered as a Communist in Santa Clara County, California, on November 8, 1936, but registered as a Democrat in 1939. According to Carol, she registered as a Communist to see what would happen and to see what the reaction would be in a small town, but regretted this move because it reflected unfavorably on her husband. She and others advised that Steinbeck was a registered Democrat and probably favored the New Deal but he had never been a Communist. (U)

This investigation also revealed that Steinbeck contributed articles to the November 8, 1936, and April 1, 1936, issues of "Pacific Weekly," cited as a Communist publication by the California Committee on Un-American Activities. He also subscribed to the "Daily People's World," west coast Communist newspaper, as of September 1939. (U) Per Army

Associates and friends of Steinbeck advised G-2 that he was honest, loyal, patriotic, and an excellent and sincere writer. They stated that although he exercised poor discretion during his early days of writing by associating with some elements of the Communist Party, he was not interested in advancing the cause of the Party but in gathering material for his writings on certain social conditions existing in the United States at that time. They reported that he wrote various articles which were published by Communist organizations because the economic views expressed were considered radical. However, he rejected Communistic political and economical theories repeatedly and discarded his association with that element when it became apparent that his prestige was being used to further interests of the Party. (G-2; 100-106188-2) (U) Per Army

<u>AFFILIATION WITH COMMUNIST FRONT ORGANIZATIONS:</u>

During 1938, Steinbeck granted the Simon J. Lubin Society of California, Inc., permission to republish his pamphlet entitled "Their Blood Is Strong," a story of the migratory agricultural workers in California, which was originally published in 1936. According to the California Committee on Un-American Activities, the Simon J. Lubin Society, Inc., was a Communist front for California agrarian penetration, organized in the Fall of 1936 by Unit 104 of the Professional Section of the Communist Party. (61-7559-S-99)

- 8 -

57

In approximately 1938, the Committee to Aid Agricultural Workers was organized under Steinbeck's leadership. Steinbeck also served as chairman of this organization which has been referred to as the John Steinbeck Committee to Aid Agricultural Workers. According to one source of unknown reliability, this committee was organized after Steinbeck had exposed the situation of the migrant farmers and "Okies" in his books. This source stated there was nothing political in the work of the committee, the purpose being to gather food and clothing for those in need. Another source indicated that the committee furnished financial assistance to the United Cannery, Agricultural, Packing and Allied Workers of America. Many of the supporters of this organization were known to be Communist Party members or people who had been active in behalf of Communist united front organizations. The American Legion Radical Research Bureau described this committee as a "very Red outfit." [redacted] Los Angeles member of the committee; 100-100188-1; 100-333317-1; 100-6833-8, p. 104; 100-3-23-16, p. 18)

John Steinbeck was one of the sponsors and delegates to the Western Writers Congress (declared to be a subsidiary of the American Writers Congress, cited by the HCUA) conference held in San Francisco, California, on November 13 and 14, 1936. (Dies Committee Hearing, Volume 3, Page 1996)

Steinbeck was active in the League of American Writers (cited by the Attorney General) during 1938-1940, serving that organization as one of the vice presidents in 1939 and as one of the board of directors of the California League of American Writers in 1940. He also furnished that organization with a statement for publication in a booklet published during May, 1938, and signed an open letter to all Senators and members of the House of Representatives during 1939. (61-7559-667812; 100-7322-8, 18; 61-7561-183110; 61-7561-2-87)

Steinbeck was among those who signed an open letter to the Government and People of the United States sponsored by the Washington Committee to Lift the Spanish Embargo (cited as a Communist front by the California Committee on Un-American Activities) on January 31, 1939. ("New York Times;" 121-23278-867112, p. 1306)

- 2 -

As of late 1940 or early 1941 the name of John Steinbeck was contained in the active indices of the National Federation for Constitutional Liberties (cited by the Attorney General). (Anonymous; 100-11170-49, p. 137)

A clipping from the "New York Times" of February 21, 1946, reported the formation in New York City of a new cooperative publishing concern, namely, Associated Magazine Contributors, Inc. The initial list of owner-contributors included John Steinbeck. Associated Magazine Contributors was cited by the California Committee on Un-American Activities when it reported that "the Communist influence is established through such news services." (123-11674-13)

In preparation for a reception to be given at the Waldorf-Astoria, New York City, on May 5, 1946, by the National Council of American-Soviet Friendship (NCASF - cited by the Attorney General) for three visiting Soviet literary figures, the Assistant to the Executive Director of the NCASF contacted Howard Fast, well-known author and probable member the Cultural Section of the Communist Party in New York City, for his approval of a list of distinguished writers, publishers, artists, and other personalities to be invited to the affair. Fast declared that naturally anti-Soviets and Trotskyites should not be invited as they would make things "very uncomfortable." According to the informant the name of John Steinbeck was among those read off to Fast which met with his approval. [redacted] 100-146964-736)

On May 27, 1946, Mrs. Muriel Draper of New York, the Chairman of the Women's Section of the American NCASF, spoke at a meeting of the Democratic Women's International Federation in Rome, Italy. In her speech she heartily agreed with the Soviet representative who had attacked United States foreign policy and reported that the American people were being given a dose of anti-Soviet propaganda worse than that against Germany before the Second World War. She stated that a number of individuals, including Steinbeck, had recently been converted to "the camp of war and anti-Sovietism." (5-28-46, "New York Herald Tribune;" 100-344442-4)

Bureau files reflect a number of instances from 1945 through 1950 wherein Steinbeck was approached by various other Communist Party front organizations to support their causes so as to enlist the widest possible mass support for their campaigns. There is no indication that he complied with these particular requests. (100-7061-983, p. 19; 100-336436-1522; 100-185087-7912; 100-370500-48)

<u>INSTANCES IN WHICH AMERICA'S ENEMIES HAVE USED OR ATTEMPTED TO USE STEINBECK'S WRITINGS AND REPUTATION TO FURTHER THEIR CAUSES:</u>

Bureau files reflect that because many of Steinbeck's writings portrayed an extremely sordid and poverty-stricken side of American life, they were reprinted in both German and Russian and used by the Nazis and Soviets as propaganda against America. (Numerous references)

An individual who had been employed during 1937 as a playwright on the Federal Theater Project, Works Progress Administration, testified before the Dies Committee that the Party told her what to write and furnished her with research material obtained from the Simon Lubin Society (previously cited). She advised that this material included some of Steinbeck's field notes in his handwriting for his book "Grapes Of Wrath." (Testimony, Rena Vale on 7-22-40; Dies Committee Executive Hearings, Volume 3, Page 1219)

Steinbeck's book, "Grapes Of Wrath," was among the periodicals and books sold from the literature table at a Communist Party May Day meeting held on May 1, 1940, in Los Angeles, California. [redacted] 61-7559-7583, p. 7) b7C b7D

A booklet announcing the courses of the Workers School of New York City, official Communist Party school, for the winter term, 1943, stated that the works of leading dramatic writers, including Steinbeck, would be used in the discussions of history of social institutions as they have been reflected by writers of all times. (1948 Report, California Committee on Un-American Activities; 100-16252-39, p. 446)

During March, 1946, a copy of a recommended reading list used by the American Youth For Democracy (cited by the Attorney General) indicated that listed books were available from the New Jersey State office of that organization at a discount. This list included Steinbeck's "The Moon Is Down."
E [redacted] state headquarters of the Communist Political Association, Newark, New Jersey; 61-777-31-60, p. 24)

<u>ASSOCIATION WITH COMMUNIST PARTY MEMBERS [illegible]</u>

On June 8, 1953, an admitted former Communist Party member (about 1937-1953) testified before the House Committee on Un-American Activities that although Steinbeck had done

- 8 -

more through his novel about the agricultural workers than anyone else for the Communist Party cause he appeared to be at odds with the Communist Party during that period although the witness could not state just how. (Roland William Kibbee, Executive Session testimony since publicly released; 61-7582-1976, p. 2330)

In letters written by Sam Darcy to Ella Winter (both Communist Party functionaries in California) during March, 1937, and November, 1940, Darcy indicated that Winter was well acquainted with Steinbeck and might have considerable influence with him. On March 7, 1937, he wrote "Needless to say, I am glad to hear about Steinbeck's new book. I hope it fulfills what you say. There is no reason why it should not. He can write, and, with the education I am told you and our friends have been giving him he ought to make the grade better than he did in his earlier book." Another undated letter obtained early in 1944 from Winter to Steinbeck indicated that Steinbeck had previously criticized Winter. This letter which was partially obscene attacked Steinbeck and indicated that he and Winter were at odds. (Highly confidential source; 100-106310-56, p. 23, 38, 99)

On June 23, 1950, Louis Budenz, former Managing Editor of the "Daily Worker," east coast Communist newspaper, and an admitted former Communist Party member, advised as follows: "Carey McWilliams is a writer, particularly noted as the author of 'Factories In The Field,' published in 1939, which was the foundation of John Steinbeck's 'Grapes Of Wrath.' When this book was published, I was advised by Alexander Trachtenberg and Jack Stachel (both Communist Party functionaries) that McWilliams was under Communist discipline. This had a great deal to do with the way we handled this book and also John Steinbeck's book because at that time McWilliams was supposedly making a Communist of Steinbeck." (Interview with Budenz; 100-338-32)

[redacted] (S)

- 6 -

[redacted] (S)

[redacted] (C)

The June 11, 1948, issue of the Los Angeles "Examiner" stated that Ring Lardner, Jr., a screen writer, had signed with Steinbeck and others to write a film version of Steinbeck's story "Pastures Of Heaven." According to the "Examiner," this "was the first Hollywood employment given any of the 'unfriendly ten' since their refusal to answer the Communist question in Washington last fall" and the move challenged the Motion Picture Association of America's announcement that none of the men cited by Congress would work until cleared of the charge. (100-235883-11, p. 5)

MISCELLANEOUS:

From time to time columnists for the "Daily Worker" and "Daily People's World" have criticized Steinbeck's writings as not portraying adequately the American Communists or supporting the American Communist movement. On the other hand these papers have also praised the books, stating in January, 1943, that he was one of the most popular authors among the Soviet Russians. Both Communists and anti-Communists criticized his 1948 series of articles for the "New York Herald Tribune" entitled "A Russian Journal," which he wrote after a visit to Russia in the Summer of 1947, as being too pro-Communist and too anti-Communist. Both sides criticized his ability to adequately portray life in Soviet Russia after such a short visit. It is noted that the articles criticized Soviet red tape and the Soviet Government but were favorable to the Russian people. (100-106224-1; 64-175-240-A; and others)

- 9 -

SECRET

During 1942, 1943, and 1944, Steinbeck was listed as one of the individuals in the United States who received Russian literature. (Office of Censorship; 65-1876-809, p. 8; 65-42085-81)

On February 23, 1944, the Steinbecks attended a reception at the Russian Embassy in Mexico City. That reception celebrated the 26th anniversary of the founding of the Russian Army. ("Novedades," morning newspaper, 2/?/44; 100-145365-17)

On August 23, 1947, Joseph Starobin, correspondent of the "Daily Worker," was in Rio de Janeiro, Brazil, conferring with leaders of the Communist Party of Brazil regarding the possibility of inviting well-known American writers to Brazil. One of the Americans recommended by Starobin was Steinbeck. There is no information available indicating Steinbeck was actually invited. [redacted] 100-51287-76, 81) ([redacted])

A Counter Intelligence Corps report of January 13, 1954, reported that there was a strong indication that the "Verlag der Nation," a publishing firm of the National Demokratische Partei (a Soviet zone political party which has been described by G-2 as "presumably a conservative party" but which is an East Zone political party and as such is Communist oriented) was about to negotiate publishing rights with seven American authors, including Steinbeck. (A usually reliable source of CIC; 100-286?0-1) (U) Per Army letter dtd 8-2-78 or 1-22-79 by 2333

SECRET

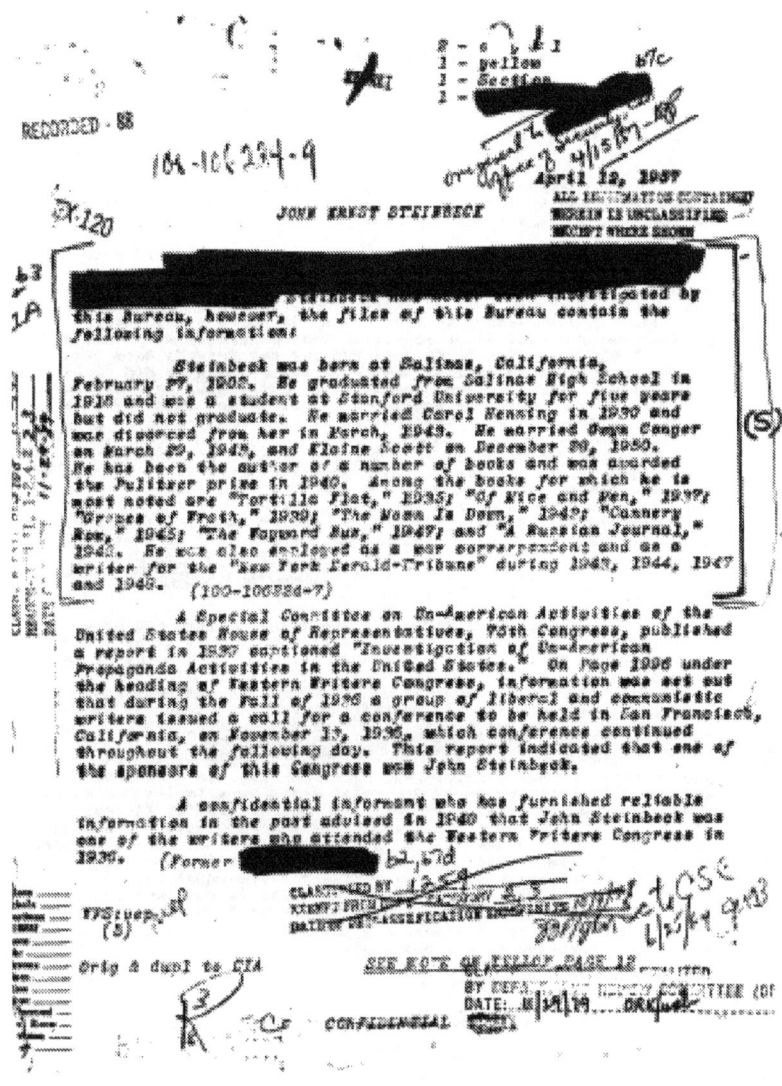

2 - ...
1 - yellow
1 - Section
1 - [redacted] b7c

RECORDED - 88

100-106224-9

April 12, 1957

ALL INFORMATION CONTAINED HEREIN IS UNCLASSIFIED EXCEPT WHERE SHOWN

JOHN ERNST STEINBECK

[redacted] Steinbeck has never been investigated by this Bureau, however, the files of this Bureau contain the following information:

Steinbeck was born at Salinas, California, February 27, 1902. He graduated from Salinas High School in 1918 and was a student at Stanford University for five years but did not graduate. He married Carol Henning in 1930 and was divorced from her in March, 1943. He married Gwyn Conger on March 29, 1943, and Elaine Scott on December 29, 1950. He has been the author of a number of books and was awarded the Pulitzer prize in 1940. Among the books for which he is most noted are "Tortilla Flat," 1935; "Of Mice and Men," 1937; "Grapes of Wrath," 1939; "The Moon Is Down," 1942; "Cannery Row," 1945; "The Wayward Bus," 1947; and "A Russian Journal," 1948. He was also employed as a war correspondent and as a writer for the "New York Herald-Tribune" during 1943, 1944, 1947 and 1948. (100-106224-7) (S)

A Special Committee on Un-American Activities of the United States House of Representatives, 75th Congress, published a report in 1937 captioned "Investigation of Un-American Propaganda Activities in the United States." On Page 1996 under the heading of Western Writers Congress, information was set out that during the Fall of 1936 a group of liberal and communistic writers issued a call for a conference to be held in San Francisco, California, on November 13, 1936, which conference continued throughout the following day. This report indicated that one of the sponsors of this Congress was John Steinbeck.

A confidential informant who has furnished reliable information in the past advised in 1940 that John Steinbeck was one of the writers who attended the Western Writers Congress in 1936. (Former [redacted] b2, b7d

CLASSIFIED BY ...
EXEMPT FROM ...
DATE OF DECLASSIFICATION INDEFINITE

WTS:uep
(5)

Orig & dupl to CIA

SEE NOTE ON YELLOW PAGE 12

BY DEPARTMENT REVIEW COMMITTEE
DATE: ...

CONFIDENTIAL

CONFIDENTIAL

JOHN ERNST STEINBECK

The Western Writers Congress was described as a communist front by the Special Committee on Un-American Activities in its report dated March 29, 1944.

A confidential informant who has furnished reliable information in the past advised in 1944 that Sam Darcy was in Russia in 1937 and that Darcy had corresponded with Ella Winter. The informant stated that a letter from Darcy in March, 1937, indicated he was pleased to hear about "Steinbeck's new book." The informant stated Darcy commented that Steinbeck could write and with the education "I am told you and our friends have been giving him, he ought to make the grade better than he did in his early book." The informant furnished no additional information to identify the Steinbeck mentioned and it is not known if this person is identical with the subject of your inquiry.
(highly confidential source; 100-18810-56 - pg 29)

The "Times-Herald," a daily newspaper published in Washington, D. C., on May 9, 1953, contained an article reflecting that Herbert A. Philbrick before a United States Senate Investigation Committee had named Ella Winter, the Australian born wife of Donald Ogden Stewart, as one of twenty-three men and women communists in Massachusetts. Additional information concerning Ella Winter Stewart was forwarded to you on June 4, 1953, in the report of Special Agent [redacted] which was dated February 18, 1953. (100-18810-A & 228)

A confidential informant who has furnished reliable information in the past advised in 1941 that Samuel Adams Darcy had stated in 1941 that he had traveled abroad in 1935 as he had been elected by the Communist Party in the United States as a representative to the Congress of the Communist International held in Moscow, Russia. Informant advised that Darcy had also returned to the United States in approximately May, 1937.
[redacted] San Francisco,*

The Committee on Un-American Activities of the United States House of Representatives, 83rd Congress, in a report captioned "Investigation of Communist Activities in the Los Angeles Area - Part 6" contains a statement of Roland William Kibbee, which he furnished to a staff member of the Committee on June 2, 1953. On Page 2379 and 2380 of the above-described report appears information which Kibbee furnished in answer to the question, "What caused your disillusionment with the Communist Party?" Kibbee stated "I can remember in my own case it even was involved more or less with the theory of the Communist Party and not outside working in organizations. . . Several of the contradictions that arose troubled me a great deal. . .

*California; 61-6599-200)

CONFIDENTIAL

CONFIDENTIAL

JOHN ERNST STEINBECK

"I remember John Steinbeck who wrote, I thought, a most effective novel about the agricultural workers in the San Joaquin Valley, or, take it a step further, that the man did more for them than anyone else. A motion picture was made of the very sorry situation that existed there. I recall that John Steinbeck was at odds with the Communist Party. I can't say just how. It was a question of hearing them attacked into work deplored and too bad he doesn't see the light, and so forth, and these things troubled me a great deal. . ." In this statement Kibbee admitted membership in the Communist Party for approximately two years beginning in approximately 1937. (61-7582-1975)

A pamphlet entitled "Their Blood Is Strong" by John Steinbeck was published in April, 1938, by the Simon J. Lubin Society of California, Incorporated. The Simon J. Lubin Society was "deeply appreciative of the cooperation received from the San Francisco News, who in October of 1936 published the seven chapters that form the bulk of this pamphlet; and especially grateful to John Steinbeck for his permission to use this material." (61-7559-2-999)

The California Committee on Un-American Activities in its report published in 1943 described the Simon J. Lubin Society, Incorporated, as a communist front for California Agrarian penetration, which was organized in the Fall of 1936 by Unit 104 of the Professional Section of the Communist Party. (California Committee 1943 report - pg 88)

On Page 148 of the same California Committee report appears information furnished by Rena M. Vale. Vale advised that the Southwest Unit of the Federal Theatre, which was composed of communists, had corresponded with the Simon J. Lubin Society in San Francisco, California, to obtain research material which that organization had turned over to John Steinbeck for his book (then unnamed) "Grapes of Wrath" and which Steinbeck had returned. She advised that when the material arrived she had examined it carefully and found notes in handwriting signed by John Steinbeck, which appeared to be field notes on migratory workers. (California Committee Report, 1943, pg. 148)

A pamphlet captioned "Writers Take Sides" was published by the League of American Writers, 381 4th Avenue, New York, New York, in May, 1938, and was described as being letters about the war in Spain from 418 American authors. On Page 56 of this pamphlet appeared a letter from John Steinbeck, the author of "Of Mice and Men" and "Tortilla Flat." (61-7561-2-87)

The "Daily Worker," an east coast communist newspaper, on April 25, 1939, contained an article captioned "Noted Writers Back Fight for Art Projects." The article reflected that 36 prominent writers, including John Steinbeck, had made public a letter urging support of the Federal Arts Project and indicated

- 3 -
CONFIDENTIAL

~~CONFIDENTIAL~~

JOHN ERNST STEINBECK

that the individuals were acting on their behalf as well as on behalf of the League of American Writers. (61-7551-183 X 10)

The "Daily Worker" of September 7, 1939, contained an article captioned "U.S. Writers League Ends Summer Session in South." The article reflected that a two-week session for student writers, which was held under the auspices of the League of American Writers had just concluded. The article described the League of American Writers as a cultural nonpartisan organization and indicated that one of the vice presidents of the organization was John Steinbeck.

The League of American Writers has been designated by the Attorney General of the United States pursuant to Executive Order 10450. (61-7559-667X12)

The records of the Department of State, State of New York, in 1941 reflected a certificate of incorporation was filed in 1939 for the League of American Writers, Incorporated. John Steinbeck, Route 1, Box 255, Los Angeles, California, was one of the directors who was appointed to act until the first annual meeting of the corporation. (100-7322-8)

The "Los Angeles Times," a daily newspaper published in Los Angeles, California, on January 23, 1941, contained an article which reflected that John Steinbeck of Los Gatos, California, was one of the California directors of the League of American Writers, which organization was dedicated to the advancement of peace and democracy as against fascism and reaction. (100-7322-16)

The report of the hearings before a Subcommittee of the Committee on Foreign Relations of the United States Senate, 81st Congress, on Page 1504 contained information attributed to "The New York Times" of January 31, 1939. The material was an open letter to the Government and people of the United States which urged that the embargo against the Spanish Republic be lifted. John Steinbeck appeared as one of the persons urging that the Spanish embargo be lifted. The article ended with a coupon which urged that all individuals fill out the coupon and forward it to the Washington Committee to Lift Spanish Embargo, Room 100, 1410 H Street, Northwest, Washington, D. C. (121-23278-267X13)

The Washington Committee to Lift Spanish Embargo was cited as a communist front in the 1948 report of the California Committee on Un-American Activities.

- 4 -

~~CONFIDENTIAL~~

CONFIDENTIAL

JOHN ERNST STEINBECK

In 1950 a confidential informant who has furnished reliable information in the past and who was an admitted member of the Communist Party until 1945 advised that Carey McWilliams was the author of the book "Factories in the Field" published in 1939, which book was the foundation of John Steinbeck's book captioned "Grapes of Wrath." The informant advised that when this book was published he had received information from Communist Party leaders that McWilliams was under communist discipline. The informant stated that this information had a great deal to do with the way the book was handled as well as Steinbeck's book, because McWilliams at that time was supposedly making a communist of Steinbeck. (Louis Budenz, concealed 400; 100-398-77)

A confidential informant who has furnished reliable information in the past advised in 1940 that the Committee to Aid Agricultural Workers was organized under the leadership of John Steinbeck, the author of "Grapes of Wrath," and that Steinbeck was chairman of the Committee. The informant stated that the Committee had the support of many prominent people in California and that in the informant's opinion, they were all people who had been active in behalf of communist united front organizations. [redacted] 100-9-23-26)

A confidential informant who has furnished reliable information in the past advised in 1941 that the name of John Steinbeck, Route 1, Box 835, Los Gatos, California, appeared in the active indices of the National Federation for Constitutional Liberties. [redacted] 100-1170-49)

A representative of another Government agency advised in 1944 that various pieces of literature published in Russia, including daily newspapers from Moscow, Russia, had arrived in the United States during 1942 and part of 1943. The informant advised that some of this material was addressed to John Steinbeck in care of Elizabeth R. Otis, 18 East 41st Street, New York, New York. [redacted] of ONI; 65-1674-308)

The United States Office of Censorship advised by letter dated July 4, 1944, that John Steinbeck, 18 East 41st Street, New York City, had received the February 18, year not given, issue of the "Moscow News," a newspaper published in Russia. (65-49005-81)

The report of the Special Committee on Un-American Activities of the United States House of Representatives,

- 5 -

CONFIDENTIAL

CONFIDENTIAL

JOHN ERNST STEINBECK

published on March 29, 1944, and captioned "Investigation of Un-American Propaganda Activities in the United States" on Page 101 contained the following: "The National Maritime Union of America, . . . has toed the Communist Party line through all its changes in recent years. (39-407-424)

"These ships of the American Merchant Marine are being supplied with libraries for the seamen to read while at sea . . . John Steinbeck's "Grapes of Wrath" is naturally present, as it would be in any Communists' selection. . ."

b1

[redacted] (S)

[redacted] (S)

[redacted] (S)

CONFIDENTIAL

CONFIDENTIAL

JOHN ERNST STEINBECK

[redacted]

A confidential informant who has furnished reliable information in the past advised in May, 1945, that the American Youth for Democracy in a list captioned "Recommended Reading List for A.Y.D." contained the book entitled "The Moon is Down" by John Steinbeck. [redacted] 786 Broad Street, Newark, N.J.; 61-777-3-60)

The American Youth for Democracy has been designated by the Attorney General of the United States pursuant to Executive Order 10450.

A confidential informant who has furnished reliable information in the past advised in 1945 that letters had been prepared to be sent to John Steinbeck, among others, requesting that he prepare a testimonial to the valiant Spanish exiles and the work of the Joint Anti-Fascist Refugee Committee. The letter requested a 75-word statement be prepared to be made a part of a leaflet and with an attached photograph it was hoped that such statements would enlist the widest possible mass support for the campaign. (Highly confidential source; 100-7061-923)

The Joint Anti-Fascist Refugee Committee has been designated by the Attorney General of the United States pursuant to Executive Order 10450.

A confidential informant who has furnished reliable information in the past advised in April, 1946, that the National Council of American-Soviet Friendship was planning to give a reception on May 2, 1946, in New York City in honor of three visiting Soviet literary figures. The informant advised that one of the persons indicated to receive an invitation to the reception was John Steinbeck, the novelist. [redacted] 100-146964-796)

The National Council of American-Soviet Friendship has been designated by the Attorney General of the United States pursuant to Executive Order 10450.

"The New York Times" on February 21, 1946, contained an article reflecting the formation of a cooperative publishing concern under the name of the Associated Magazine Contributors,

- 7 -

CONFIDENTIAL

CONFIDENTIAL

JOHN ERNST STEINBECK

Incorporated. The article set forth the initial list of member contributors, which included the name of John Steinbeck. (123-11874-19)

The 1948 report of the California Committee on Un-American Activities reflected that in addition to completely communist-controlled and dominated publications there was also a long list of Trade Union, racial, minority, liberal and special interests publications into which communists had infiltrated. The report reflected that the communist influence was established through such news services as the Associated Magazine Contributors, Incorporated, and others. (100-13252-39 - pg 39)

[redacted] (S)

The October [illegible], 1947, "Daily Worker," an east coast communist newspaper, published an article captioned "Found Soviets Eager for Peace, Capa, Steinbeck Tell Trib Forum." This article indicated that Capa read a joint report by himself and John Steinbeck at the Herald Tribune Forum. This report purportedly stated that the Russian people were destroyed and hurt much more than any others that they, Capa and Steinbeck, had seen during their many years on the battle fields. The report further indicated that the Russian masses would strongly approve the halt of the "vicious and insane games" of recrimination between Russia and the U.S. It was indicated that the Russians were particularly interested in hearing about "the persecution of liberals" in America. (100-106224)

The "Daily Worker" on April 16, 1948, contained a book review of John Steinbeck's "A Russian Journal," which was described as being a book containing photographs by Robert Capa, which had been published by the Viking Press in New York, New York. The article reflected "John Steinbeck's warm sympathy for people, as evidenced in his 'A Russian Journal,' (published today) is the one positive feature of an account of a visit to the Soviet Union which is otherwise overrun with frivolous provincialism and a coy disinclination to face political realities. . .

CONFIDENTIAL

CONFIDENTIAL

JOHN ERNST STEINBECK

"What is one to say of a writer to whom the distinctive characteristic of American capitalist society is that it provides a government of 'checks and balances'? Or of the naivete which has it that 'our government is designed to keep anyone from getting too much power or, having got it, from keeping it'? And, 'we agreed,' Steinbeck writes solemnly, 'that this makes our country function more slowly, but that it certainly makes it function more surely....'

"One could go on quoting Steinbeck, but what for? A Russian Journal is much more enlightening about the kind of culture which develops such intellectual Sad Sackery than about the Soviet Union..."

The "New Leader," a weekly magazine, on August 21, 1948, contained an article captioned "Steinbeck Sans Wrath," which was a book review of "A Russian Journal," which was written by Steinbeck and contained pictures by Robert Capa. The article reflected that "Mr. Steinbeck has joined the fraternity of weeks visitors. For three weeks he toured the Soviet Union under the subtle guidance of VOKS, the government agency for 'cultural liaison,'..." The article reflected he had attended the "celebration of the 800th anniversary of Moscow with Louis Aragon, the French Stalinist writer" and had visited the country home of "such Soviet millionaires as Alexander Korneichuk – and concludes that the Russians have plenty to eat; he even states that the quality of Russian clothing improved during the few weeks he spent in Russia..."

The article further reflected "most startling, perhaps, is Steinbeck's own attitude toward the Soviet Union. His book is full of what Koestler would call false equations. When Capa is stopped from taking pictures at a lend-leased tractor plant in Stalingrad, Steinbeck reminds us that foreigners may not photograph Oak Ridge either. In his mind 'Moscowitis' and 'Washingtonitis' cancel each other out. When he admits that the collective farm he was shown put on a big show for him, he insists that 'any Kansas farmer' would do the same for his guests...

"Steinbeck used to be known as a man with a strong social conscience. 'The Grapes of Wrath' and 'Tortilla Flat' were full of righteous moral indignation about social and economic injustice. In 'The Moon is Down' Steinbeck made a heated if somewhat pedestrian

- 9 -

CONFIDENTIAL

CONFIDENTIAL

JOHN ERNST STEINBECK

attack on totalitarian aggression and conquest. Those were the days when Steinbeck could be counted upon to stand up and wield his pen in behalf of democracy and freedom. Even today had he gone to Spain or China, he would surely not have come back to write a book in order to demonstrate that the 'Chinese people want good lives and comfort' or that 'the Spaniards like peace.' "

A confidential informant who has furnished reliable information in the past advised in 1948 that the firm of World Video, Incorporated, was chartered in New York State on December 18, 1947, and that the firm prepared television programs. The officers of the firm include John Steinbeck as vice president and Robert Capa as assistant vice president. [redacted] NYC; 100-340928-111]

The "New York Herald-Tribune" of May 18, 1948, contained an article captioned "Women's Rally in Rome Hears Russia Praised." The article, which was datelined Rome, May 17, reflected that the meeting was that of the Democratic Women's International Federation, whose aim was to fight "American, British and French imperialists and warmongers." The article reflected that the chief American delegate, Mrs. Muriel Draper, chairman of the women's section of the American National Committee for American-Soviet Friendship mentioned several persons converted to "the camp of war and anti-Sovietism," which included John Steinbeck.

The "Los Angeles Examiner," a daily newspaper published in Los Angeles, California, on June 11, 1948, contained an article reflecting that Ring Lardner, Jr., had signed a contract with John Steinbeck and others to write a film version of Steinbeck's story "Pastures of Heaven." The article reflected this was the first Hollywood employment given "one of the 'un-friendly ten' since their refusal to answer the Communist question in Washington last fall." (100-295665-11)

The "Daily Worker" on April 1, 1955, contained an article captioned "John Steinbeck Takes a Look at Moscow and

- 19 -

CONFIDENTIAL

CONFIDENTIAL

JOHN ERNST STEINBECK

'Death of a Racket.' " The article was a review of an article by Steinbeck which appeared in the April 2, 1955, issue of "Saturday Review." The article reflected that Steinbeck's article captioned "Death of a Racket" was based on the book "False Witness" written by Harvey Matusow. Steinbeck's article reportedly stated:

"The Matusow testimony to anyone who will listen places a bouquet of forget-me-nots on the grave of McCarthy. The ridiculousness of the whole series of investigations now becomes apparent, even to what a friend of mine used to call peanut-munchers. Matusow will have a much greater effect than he knows. What follows cannot be worse and may be better. It will surely be funny."

The "Daily Worker" article continues, "It is impossible not to be moved by this kind of statement of an angered scorn which, if the record is to be kept straight, itself participated in, and helped to create, that very climate, those same 'winds of the time' as Steinbeck puts it, 'when certain basic nonsense was allowed to pass unnoticed.' For Steinbeck was taken in too by the Cold War leadership to such an extent that he did not scruple even to lend the authority of his literary achievement to State Department broadcasts in fascist Spain, Italy, Vienna, etc."

The article continued "Steinbeck's contempt for the 'certain basic nonsense' which was believed under the influence of the Cold War hysteria does not lead him to a rejection of the Big Lie about the working-class Communist Party. He still says that the Communists approve of 'the climate of disunity and suspicion which has haunted us for the last few years,' and that Communists 'would much rather keep the investigations going with their harvest of fear and disruption.' . . . It suffices that John Steinbeck has expressed sentiments which a literary artist with a sense of responsibility for his nation cannot long silence without crushing his talent. . ." (100-374955-A)

For additional information concerning Steinbeck you may desire to contact the Assistant Chief of Staff, Intelligence, of the United States Army and the Department of State.

The above information is furnished to you as a result of your request for a name check and should not be construed as a clearance or nonclearance of captioned individual. The information is furnished for your use and should not be disseminated outside of your agency.

- 11 -

CONFIDENTIAL

CONFIDENTIAL SECRET

SECRET

JOHN ERNST STEINBECK

NOTE:

Steinbeck never investigated by Bureau. Steinbeck sent letter to Attorney General Biddle in 1942 which contained "Do you suppose you could ask Edgar's boys to stop stepping on my heels? They think I'm an enemy alien. Its getting tiresome." The AG was advised on 5/21/42 that Steinbeck was not being and had never been investigated.

The Attorney General's office telephonically requested the Bureau's file on Steinbeck on 10/27/42 and was advised only information available was two pamphlets. G-2 investigated Steinbeck in 1943 and it was recommended Steinbeck not be given Army Commission. (100-106224) (C)(U) Per Army Letter dtd 8-2-78 #WI-33-79 2333 GAO/bjm

- 32 -

CONFIDENTIAL SECRET

SECRET

97

ALL INFORMATION CONTAINED HEREIN IS UNCLASSIFIED EXCEPT WHERE SHOWN OTHERWISE

Mr. Tolson
Mr. Belmont
Mr. Mohr
Mr. Callahan
Mr. Conrad
Mr. DeLoach
Mr. Evans
Mr. Malone
Mr. Rosen
Mr. Sullivan
Mr. Tavel
Mr. Trotter
Tele. Room
Mr. Ingram
Miss Gandy

September 13, 1961

Mr. DeLoach:

RE: MENTION OF FBI IN THE BOOK "THE WINTER OF OUR DISCONTENT" BY JOHN STEINBECK

The above book, a recent Literary Guild selection, is a novel laid in the fictitious town of New Baytown, New York, and concerns the problems of a young grocery store clerk whose family had at one time been among the leaders of the community. The book is written in the first-person as though being told by the "hero." At the beginning of the book he describes various persons of the town including one Stonewall Jackson Smith, the Chief of Police, whom he characterizes as being of above average intelligence for the town and who "even took the FBI training at Washington, D. C."

Later in the story, just a weekend before the local elections, the Grand Jury indicts the city manager and other high officials for corruption, etc. Immediately prior to the announcement of the indictments, Chief "Stoney" Smith had made a trip to the State Capitol and in a subsequent conversation between the Chief and the grocer clerk, in which the Chief is clearly suffering from a guilty conscience, it becomes evident that he has been excluded from the indictments because he chose to "turn state's evidence," so to speak, and furnish information against the other town officials.

REC- 38

SEP 21 1961

OBSERVATION

While Steinbeck does not belabor the fact that the Chief of Police is FBI trained, nevertheless a careful reader cannot fail to recall the reference in the initial introduction to the Chief when his behavior concerning the indictments comes up.

By contrast, Steinbeck's references to a Justice Department investigator who appears in the story investigating the illegal entry into the United States of one of the townspeople are of the highest caliber.

RECOMMENDATION

For information.

1961

ULG:kmd

M. A. Jones

TOP SECRET

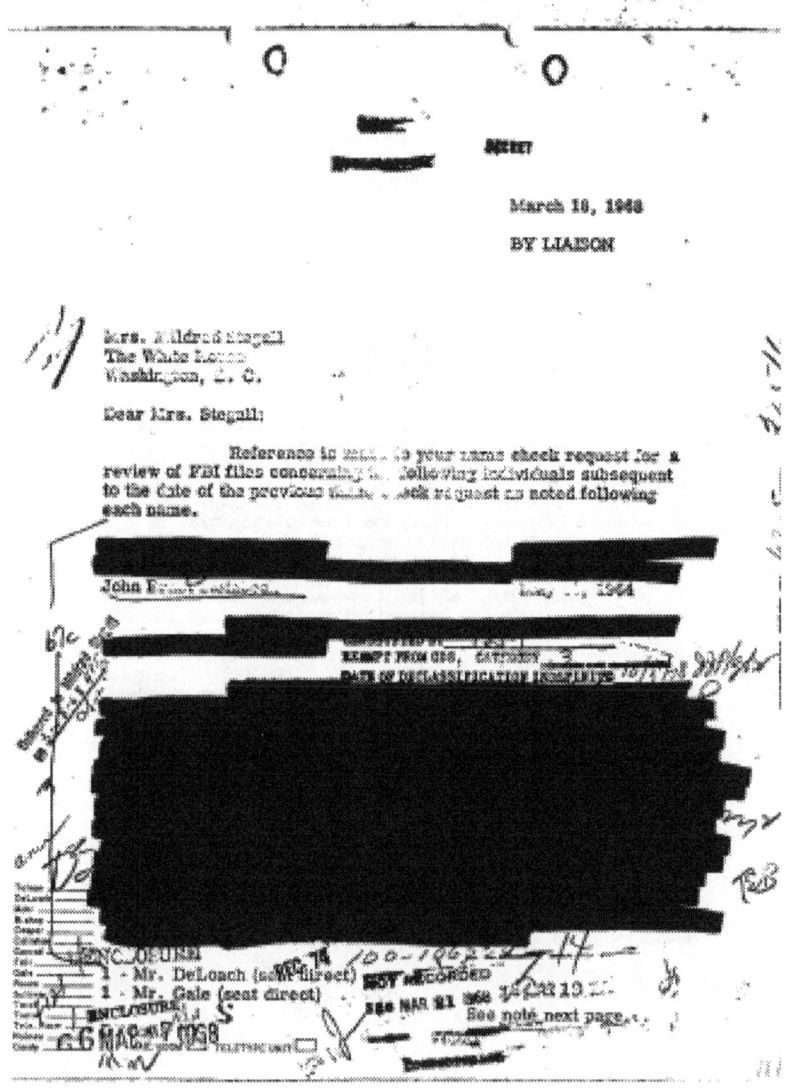

SECRET

March 18, 1968

BY LIAISON

Mrs. Mildred Stegall
The White House
Washington, D. C.

Dear Mrs. Stegall:

Reference is made to your name check request for a review of FBI files concerning the following individuals subsequent to the date of the previous name check request as noted following each name.

[redacted]

John [illegible] May [illegible], 1964

[redacted]

EXEMPT FROM GDS, CATEGORY 3
DATE OF DECLASSIFICATION INDEFINITE

[redacted]

ENCLOSURE
1 - Mr. DeLoach (sent direct)
1 - Mr. Gale (sent direct)

NOT RECORDED

See note next page.

Mrs. Mildred Stegall

b7C [redacted] (U)

The files of the Identification Division were checked and found to contain no additional pertinent data concerning the above individuals.

A copy of this communication has not been sent to the Attorney General.

Sincerely yours,

- 2 -

NOTE: Our files reflect that the final results of our name check concerning [redacted] were sent by memorandum dated 9-12-63, rather than 9-4-63. The additional information was developed subsequent to the prior summary memorandum furnished in 1963.

b7C

SECRET

ALL INFORMATION CONTAINED
HEREIN IS UNCLASSIFIED
EXCEPT WHERE SHOWN
OTHERWISE

May 20, 1964

JOHN ERNST STEINBECK- Summary

John Ernst Steinbeck has never been the subject of investigation by the FBI.

Mr. Steinbeck was born at Salinas, California, on February 27, 1902. He was a student at Stanford University for five years but did not graduate. He married Carol Henning in 1930 and was divorced from her in March, 1943. He married Gwyn Conger on March 29, 1943, and Elaine Scott on December 28, 1950. He has been the author of a number of books and was awarded the Pulitzer prize in 1940. He was also employed as a war correspondent and as a writer for the "New York Herald Tribune" during 1943, 1946, 1947 and 1948.

According to the annual report of the House of Representatives Committee on Un-American Activities published in 1939, during the Fall of 1936 a group of liberal and communist writers issued a call for a conference to be held in San Francisco, California, on November 13, 1936, under the auspices of the Western Writers' Congress. The report indicated that one of the sponsors of this Congress was John Steinbeck. A reliable informant of the FBI advised in 1943 that John Steinbeck was one of the writers who attended the Western Writers' Congress in 1936. In 1944, this Congress was described by the House Committee on Un-American Activities (HCUA) as a communist front.

According to a reliable informant of the FBI, Sam Darcy, in 1937, indicated to Ella Winter that he was pleased to hear about "Steinbeck's new book." Darcy commented that Steinbeck could write and, with the education "I am told you and our friends have been giving him, he ought to make the grade better than he did in his early book." The informant furnished no additional information to identify the Steinbeck mentioned, and it is not known if this person is identical with John Ernst Steinbeck. (X) U

CLASSIFIED BY
EXEMPT FROM GDS, CATEGORY
DATE OF DECLASSIFICATION INDEFINITE

[redacted]

CJH:smg/ear
(10)

ENCLOSURE

SECRET ENCLOSURE

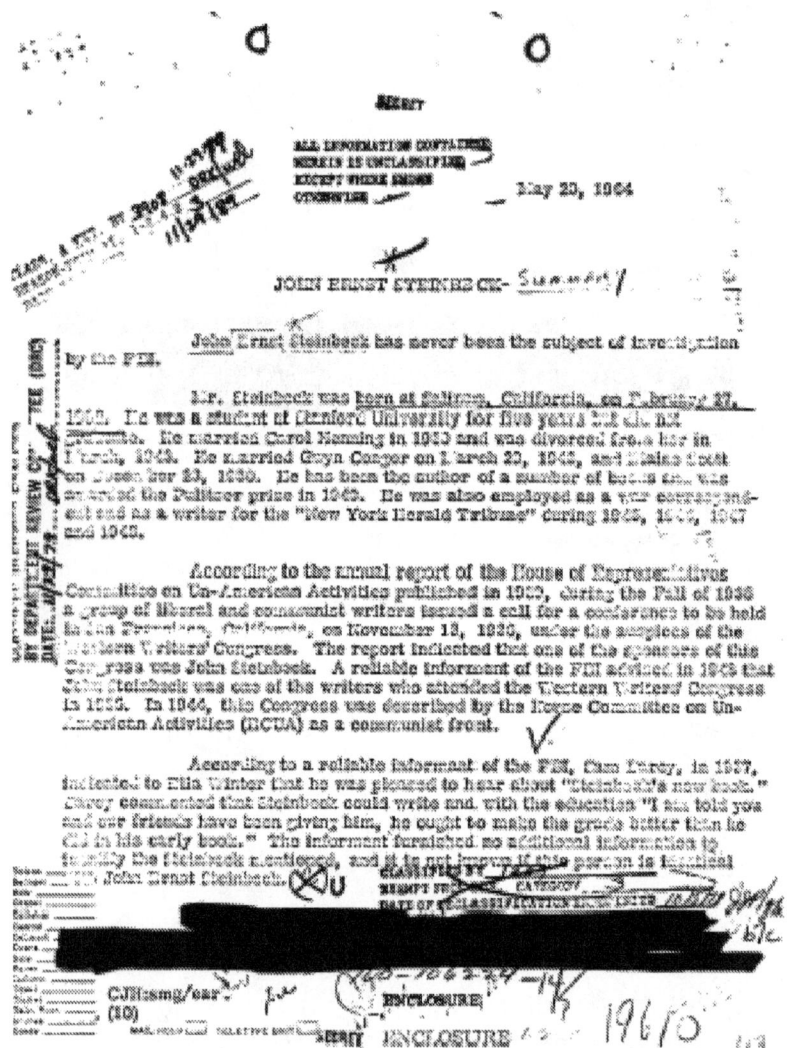

[redacted]

A pamphlet entitled "Their Blood Is Strong" by John Steinbeck was published in April, 1938, by the Simon J. Lubin Society of California, Incorporated (SJLSCI). This pamphlet consisted of material which Steinbeck had published elsewhere and which had been reprinted in pamphlet form with Steinbeck's permission. The California Committee on Un-American Activities (CCUA) in its report published in 1943 described the SJLSCI as a communist front for California agrarian penetration.

A pamphlet captioned "Writers Take Sides" was published by the League of American Writers (LAW), New York, New York, in May, 1938, and was described as containing letters about the war in Spain from 418 American authors. On Page 56 of this pamphlet there appeared a letter from John Steinbeck. The "Daily Worker," an East coast communist newspaper, on April 23, 1938, contained an article noting that 33 prominent writers, including John Steinbeck, had made publ a letter urging support of the Federal Arts Project and indicating that the individuals were acting on their behalf as well as on the behalf of the LAW. The article notes th one of the vice presidents of the organization was John Steinbeck.

The records of the Department of State, State of New York, in 1941 reflected a certificate of incorporation was filed in 1939 for the LAW. John Steinbeck, of Los Angeles, California, was one of the directors who was appointed t act until the first annual meeting of the corporation.

The LAW has been cited as subversive pursuant to Executive Order 10450.

The report of the hearings before a subcommittee of the Committee on Foreign Relations of the United States Senate, 81st Congress, on Page 1534, contained information attributed to "The New York Times" of January 21, 1949, which consisted of an open letter urging that the embargo against Spain be lifted. John Steinbeck appeared as one of the persons urging that the Spanish embargo be lifted, and it was indicated that the organization sponsoring the plea was the Washington Committee to Lift Spanish Embargo. This organization was cited as a communist front in the 1948 report of the CCUA.

In 1950, a reliable informant of the FBI advised that Carey McWillia was the author of the book, "Factories in the Field," published in 1939, which was the foundation of John Steinbeck's book, "Grapes of Wrath." According to the informant, McWilliams was under communist discipline and this had a great deal to do with the way this book was handled as well as Steinbeck's book because McWillia at that time was supposedly making a communist out of Steinbeck.

- 2 -

In 1940, a reliable informant of the FBI advised that the Committee To Aid Agricultural Workers was organized under the leadership of John Steinbeck, and it had the support of many prominent people in California. In the informant's opinion, they were all people who had been active in behalf of "communist united front organizations."

In 1941, a reliable source advised the FBI that the name of John Steinbeck, Los Gatos, California, appeared in the active indices of the National Federation for Constitutional Liberties. This organization has been cited as subversive pursuant to Executive Order 10450.

In 1944, the records of the Office of Naval Intelligence indicated that one John Steinbeck, New York, New York, had received literature and daily newspapers from Moscow, Russia, during 1942 and 1943. The United States Office of Censorship advised in 1944 that this same John Steinbeck had received a copy of the "Moscow News," a newspaper published in Russia.

The report of the House of Representatives Committee on Un-American Activities, published on March 29, 1944, described The National Maritime Union of America as having "toed the Communist Party line through all its changes in recent years." The report continued, "These ships of the American Merchant Marine are being supplied with libraries for the seamen to read while at sea...John Steinbeck's 'Grapes of Wrath' is naturally present, as it would be in any Communists' selection."

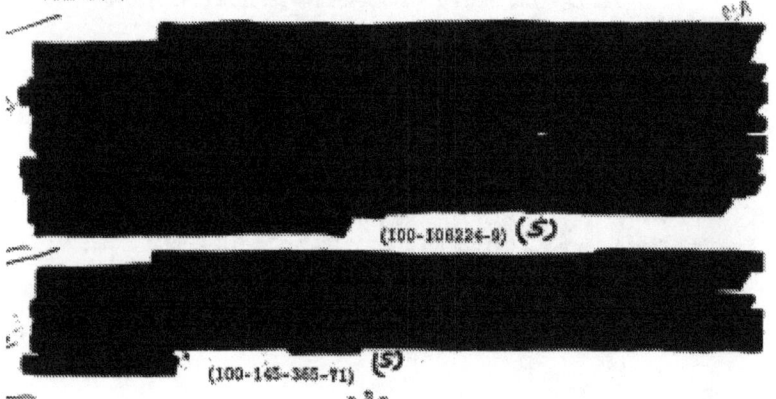

[redacted] (100-108224-9) (S)

[redacted] (100-145-365-71) (S)

- 3 -

A reliable informant of the FBI advised in May, 1945, that the American Youth for Democracy, an organization which has been cited as subversive within the purview of Executive Order 10450, issued a list of recommended reading which contained the book entitled "The Moon is Down" by John Steinbeck.

In 1945, a reliable informant of the FBI advised that letters had been prepared to be sent to John Steinbeck, among others, requesting that he prepare a testimonial to the "valiant Spanish exiles and the work of the Joint Anti-Fascist Refugee Committee." This organization has been cited as subversive within the purview of Executive Order 10450.

A reliable source, in April, 1946, advised the FBI that the National Council of American-Soviet Friendship in New York City was planning to give a reception in New York City in honor of three visiting Soviet literary figures. According to the informant, John Steinbeck was indicated to be one of those persons who would receive an invitation to attend this reception.

"The New York Times," on February 21, 1946, described the formation of a cooperative publishing concern under the name of the Associated Magazine Contributors, Incorporated. The article set forth the initial list of owner-contributors, which included the name of John Steinbeck. The 1946 report of the CCUA discussed communist infiltration of various publications. The report reflected that communist influence was established through such news services as the Associated Magazine Contributors, Incorporated, and others.

[redacted]

The October 24, 1947, issue of the "Daily Worker" contained an article concerning a report which had been read at the Herald Tribune Forum. John Steinbeck was coauthor of this report. The report expressed sympathy for the sufferings of the Russian people during the war and indicated that the Russian masses would strongly approve the halt of the "vicious and insane games" of recrimination between Russia and the United States.

The "Daily Worker" on April 16, 1948, contained a book review of John Steinbeck's "A Russian Journal." The article stated, "John Steinbeck's warm sympathy for people, as evidenced in his 'A Russian Journal,' (published today) is the one positive feature of an account of a visit to the Soviet Union which is otherwise over run with frivolous provincialism and a coy disinclination to face political realities."

- 6 -

This article continued to criticize Steinbeck for his favorable references to the American form of government, including his statements that "our government is designed to keep anyone from getting too much power or, having got it, from keeping it," and "we agreed that this makes our country function more slowly, but that it certainly makes it function more surely."

The "New Leader," a weekly magazine, on August 21, 1948, also reviewed Steinbeck's "A Russian Journal" and criticized Steinbeck as a Soviet apologist. The article indicated that Steinbeck had visited the homes of millionaires and implied that from this Steinbeck had concluded that the Russians have plenty to eat and that the quality of Russian clothing had improved. The article noted that Steinbeck constantly made excuses for the Russians, and it pointed out that when he admitted that a collective farm had put on a big show for him, he also insisted that "any Kansas farmer" would do the same for his guests.

The "New York Herald Tribune" of May 16, 1948, contained an article concerning a meeting in Rome, Italy, of the Democratic Women's International Federation whose aim was to fight "American, British and French imperialists and warmongers." At this meeting, John Steinbeck was publicly criticized as one of several persons who had been converted to "the camp of war and anti-Sovietism."

The "Los Angeles Examiner," on June 11, 1948, contained an article reflecting that Ring Lardner, Jr., had signed a contract with John Steinbeck and others to write a film version of Steinbeck's story, "Pastures of Heaven." The article reflected that this was the first Hollywood employment given "any of the 'un-friendly ten' since their refusal to answer the communist question in Washington last fall."

The "Daily Worker," on April 1, 1955, contained an article, "John Steinbeck Takes a Look at Matusow and 'Death of a Racket.'" The article was a review of an article Steinbeck had prepared concerning the book, "False Witness," written by Harvey Matusow. The Steinbeck article was obviously critical of Matusow and stated that as a result of Matusow's testimony, the "ridiculousness of the whole series of the investigations now becomes apparent." The "Daily Worker" article was critical of Steinbeck, especially when he asserted that the communists approved of "the climate of disunity and suspicion which has haunted us for the last few years," and that the communists "would much rather keep the investigations going with their harvest of fear and disruption." (100-106224-9)

SECRET

In 1959, a reliable source advised the FBI that John Steinbeck was on the mailing list of the Japan Council Against Atomic and Hydrogen Bombs. Another reliable source has described this organization as a communist infiltrated organization in Japan. (105-62460-14)

In 1959, a reliable source advised the FBI that during July of that year John Steinbeck, in care of McIntosh and Otis, Inc., New York, New York, had been paid the sum of $108.70 from the New York account of the National Bank of Bulgaria. It was not known to the source if this individual was identical with John Ernst Steinbeck. (65-34794-239)

In April, 1964, a reliable source advised the FBI that on March 12, 1964, John Ernst Steinbeck had received the sum of $420 as an author's fee from the Soviet publication, "Novyi Mir." (65-28939-3046)

[redacted] (S)

- 6 -

SECRET

About the editor . . .

Thomas Fensch is the author or editor of over 25 books of nonfiction published since 1970. Some of his books include:

Steinbeck and Covici:
The Story of a Friendship

Conversations with John Steinbeck

Conversations with James Thurber

The Man Who Was Walter Mitty:
The Life and Work of James Thurber

The Man Who Was Dr. Seuss:
The Life and Work of Theodor Geisel

Of Sneethes and Whos and the
Good Dr. Seuss:
Essays on the Writings and
Life of Theodor Geisel

Oskar Schindler and His List:
The Man, the Book, the Film,
the Holocaust and Its Survivors

. . . and many others.

Thomas Fensch is the editor of the Top Secret series and publisher of New Century Books. He holds a doctorate from Syracuse University and lives in southern New Mexico.

www.ingramcontent.com/pod-product-compliance
Lightning Source LLC
Chambersburg PA
CBHW032045150426
43194CB00006B/433